JOHANN WOLFGANG von GOETHE

Born in Frankfurt in 1749, Goethe enjoyed a long and varied creative life, writing poetry, novels and essays as well as drama. His early plays, notably *Götz von Berlichingen*, first staged in Berlin in 1794, were influenced by Shakespeare and led the way for the young Sturm und Drang writers. Then came a more classical phase, typified by *Egmont* and *Torquato Tasso*, both first staged at Weimar, where from 1791 to 1817 Goethe was director of the Court theatre – a post he shared for some years with fellow dramatist Friedrich Schiller. The first part of *Faust* was published in 1808 and performed complete in 1829. The second part was published in 1832, the year of Goethe's death in Weimar, and not staged until 1854.

HOWARD BRENTON

Born in Portsmouth in 1942 and educated at Cambridge University, Howard Brenton has written well over twenty stage plays as well as translations, adaptations and screenplays. His best-known theatre work includes *Christie in Love*, *Bloody Poetry*, *The Churchill Play* (twice revived by the Royal Shakespeare Company), and, for the National Theatre, *Weapons of Happiness*, *The Romans in Britain*, *Pravda* (co-written with David Hare) and translations of *The Life of Galileo* and *Danton's Death*. More recently there have been two collaborations with Tariq Ali: *Iranian Nights* at the Royal Court Theatre and *Moscow Gold* for the RSC. *Berlin Bertie* was seen both at the Royal Court and the Deutsches Theater, Berlin, who have commissioned his next piece, *One Once*. He has also written a novel, *Diving for Pearls*, and *Hot Irons*, a volume of essays and diaries.

Other Classics in Translation

Anton Chekhov
THE SEAGULL
UNCLE VANYA
tr. Pam Gems

Anton Chekhov
THREE SISTERS
tr. Stephen Mulrine

Jean Cocteau
LES PARENTS TERRIBLES
    (INDISCRETIONS)
tr. Jeremy Sams

Corneille
THE ILLUSION
tr. Tony Kushner

Euripides
MEDEA
*tr. Kenneth McLeish &
    Frederic Raphael*

Henrik Ibsen
A DOLL'S HOUSE
HEDDA GABLER
PEER GYNT
tr. Kenneth McLeish

Henrik Ibsen
AN ENEMY OF THE
    PEOPLE
tr. Arthur Miller

Federico Garcia Lorca
BLOOD WEDDING &
    YERMA
*tr. Langston Hughes & WS
    Mervin*

Molière
THE HYPOCHONDRIAC
tr. Martin Sorrell

Alfred de Musset
FANTASIO AND OTHER
    PLAYS
various translators

Edmond Rostand
CYRANO DE BERGERAC
tr. Anthony Burgess

Seneca
THYESTES
tr. Caryl Churchill

August Strindberg
MISS JULIE
tr. Kenneth McLeish

JOHANN WOLFGANG VON GOETHE

FAUST

PARTS I & II

A NEW VERSION BY
HOWARD BRENTON

FROM A LITERAL TRANSLATION BY
CHRISTA WEISMAN

NICK HERN BOOKS
London

A Nick Hern Book

This version of Goethe's *Faust* first published in Great Britain
in 1995 as a paperback original by Nick Hern Books,
14 Larden Road, London W3 7ST, by arrangement with
the Royal Shakespeare Company

Faust Parts I and II copyright in this version © 1995
by Howard Brenton

Introduction copyright © 1995 by Howard Brenton

Front cover illustration by Nick Higgins

Typeset by Country Setting, Woodchurch, Kent TN26 3TB
Printed by Cox and Wyman Ltd, Reading, Berks

A CIP catalogue record for this book is available from
the British Library

ISBN 1 85459 204 1

A Note on the Text

This version of *Faust* was prepared for a production by the
Royal Shakespeare Company. The aim was to make cuts which
preserved Goethe's vision and dramaturgy, but which made each
part a play of around three hours' length. Most of the cuts have
been made in Part Two, which is a hugely complex poem, half-in
and half-out of the theatre: the original is about twice as long as
the text printed here. In rehearsal there were further cuts, but
I have restored some passages for this edition, where I felt that,
though perhaps dramatically slack, they are fascinating to read.

Michael Bogdanov, the play's director, prepared a cut version of
the original German text, which Christa Weisman then translated
into an un-rhymed, unscanned literal version, deliberately void of
any literary value but linguistically accurate. My job was to take
courage, and a six-month-long deep breath, and to try to write
Goethe's great play/poem in my own language.

HB

Dramatis Personae

Part One

DIRECTOR
POET
ACTOR
THE LORD
MEPHISTOPHELES
THE ANGEL RAPHAEL
THE ANGEL GABRIEL
FAUST
THE EARTH SPIRIT
WAGNER, *a student*
A BEGGAR
OLD PEASANT
BRANDER, SIEBEL, FROSCH, ALTMAYER (*drinkers*)
A MALE MONKEY
A FEMALE MONKEY
AN OLD WITCH
MARGARETA (GRETCHEN)
MARTHA (GRETCHEN*'s neighbour*)
LIESCHEN
VALENTIN (GRETCHEN*'s brother*)
A WILL-O'-THE-WISP
WITCHES
A HALF-WITCH
A GENERAL
A POLITICIAN
A PARVENU
AN AUTHOR
A PEDLAR-WITCH
LILITH (ADAM*'s wife)*
A YOUNG WITCH
AN OLD WITCH

Heavenly hosts, choir of angels, students,
soldiers, citizens, animals, monkeys

Part Two

ARIEL
FAUST
COURTIERS
THE EMPEROR
SQUIRES
MEPHISTOPHELES
CHANCELLOR
COMMANDER-IN-CHIEF
TREASURER
SENESCHAL
ASTROLOGER
HERALD
'FEAR', 'HOPE', 'PRUDENCE' (*allegories in the carnival*)
A DRUNKARD
'BOY CHARIOTEER', 'STARVELING', 'MEANNESS'
(*allegories on* MEPHISTOPHELES' *chariot at the carnival*)
CHATTERING WOMEN
NYMPHS
PAGES
CHAMBERLAIN
STANDARD-BEARER
A FOOL
BLONDE WOMAN
BRUNETTE WOMAN
AN ARCHITECT
LADIES OF THE COURT
A KNIGHT
A DIPLOMAT
A DUENNA
A PROFESSOR
PARIS
HELEN OF TROY
A COURTIER
A POET
WAGNER (*now older*)
HOMUNCULUS
SPHINXES
GRIFFINS
SIRENS
THE LAMIAE
EMPUSA
MENELAUS
LYNCEUS

EUPHORION (*child of* FAUST *and* HELEN OF TROY)
A YOUNG GIRL
SMASH-ALL, GRAB-ALL, KEEP-ALL, SPEEDY-LOOT
(*scavengers on a battlefield*)
GUARDS
ARCHBISHOP
A WAYFARER
BAUCIS (*an old woman*)
PHILEMON (*her husband, also old*)
THREE MIGHTY MEN
WANT, DEBT, NEED, CARE (*the 'four grey women'*)
LEMURS
DOCTOR MARIANUS
MATER GLORIOSA
BLESSED BOYS
Soldiers, chorus of women prisoners, princes,
devils, anchorites, chorus of angels

This version of *Faust* was first performed by the
Royal Shakespeare Company at the Swan Theatre,
Stratford-upon-Avon, on 2 September 1995 with the following
company of actors, all of whom played several parts, with the
exception of those playing Faust and Mephistopheles:

Tilly Blackwood, Kate Duchêne, Sophie Heyman,
Josie Lawrence, Melissa Lloyd, Jules Melvin,
Sheila Steafel, Anita Wright

Nick Cavaliere, Paul Chahidi, Timothy Davies, Jeffery Dench,
John Dougall, Michael Feast (*Faust*), Christopher Godwin,
James Hayes, Peter Holdway, Hugh Quarshie (*Mephistopheles*),
Christopher Tune, Zubin Varla, Godfrey Walters

Directed by Michael Bogdanov
Set designed by Chris Dyer
Costumes designed by Kendra Ullyart
Music by John Cameron

FAUST

PART ONE

1. Prologue in the Theatre

DIRECTOR You two,
                We've stuck together
          In the theatre,
          Despite the stress
                Of life in our profession:
          The disastrous openings,
          The critical pannings and the odd success.
                But I've a confession:
          This time around,
                I don't know.
          I feel that we're on dodgy ground.
          How do we make this show
                About life and death
          Funny and philosophical
                In the same breath?
          How do we make
                Redemption entertaining?
          I love to see an audience
                Pour into the theatre,
          A river, floodwater
                In a whirlpool in the foyer,
          Fighting for a ticket and a drink:
                A wave that rises then falls
          Crashing into the stalls.
                What will they all think?
          Only you, the poet, can unite
                So many different thoughts,
          Feelings, dreams.
                My friend,
          We need a big one tonight.

POET   Don't talk to me of theatre-goers,
                That socially inadequate herd:
          The pretentious nerd
          In the gallery,
                The glamorous nonentity

In the stalls.
                    Poetic inspiration panics
At the stink of gin and tonics;
The moment's fashion
                    Glitters then fades away;
True poetry, true passion,
                    Must wait to have its day.

ACTOR   Ah, writing for posterity!
                    I say
Just knock out the play
                    In the here and now;
Don't worry if you're a poet or a hack.
The bigger the audience
                    the better the come-back.
OK let's have reason, common sense,
                    The beautiful and true:
But with a bit of a gag and a giggle too.

DIRECTOR   And ram it home: spectacles,
Big effects, big sets,
Glamour and rippling pectorals,
Let the mob
                    Have it,
Wallop! Why not?
I get sick of art,
                    I get sick
Of breaking my heart
With ambiguity and difficulty;
I know exactly how I can
                    Make myself a popular man:
Stick
                    The lot on the stage;
Let purists rage,
                    Just chuck it all in:
Sentiment, sex and the Sunday joint,
                    Give 'em a rich stew.
What's the point
Of highly wrought but thin,
                    Bitterly complex
Plays for the few?

POET   But you well know that's a recipe
                    For made-to-order, clichéd

'Popular' drama;
　　　　It's a maxim of yours to hate
Writing that exploits the second rate.

DIRECTOR   A formula
　　　　　　That's popular
Doesn't worry me.
You've got to remember
　　　　　Who comes to see
A play, whom it's for:
This one's got a one-act bladder;
This one's madder
　　　　　Than anything on the stage;
This one's a bore
　　　　　With a mind made up
By the critics' page.
So, happiness is a full house?
Look again at the customers:
The smooth, and the somewhat rougher,
The persistent
　　　　　Cougher,
The likely lad out for an aftershow whirl
　　　　　With a working girl,
The alki out of his head.
I tell you, do anything, surprise
　　　　　'Em, hit 'em
Between the eyes;
Don't and we . . . are . . . dead.
What's the matter? What have I said?

POET   Go and look for another
　　　　　Potboiling slave:
A real writer can't throw away
The talent that nature gave.
What gives words the power to tear apart
　　　　　The human heart?
What weaves the flowery charms
　　　　　That tempt the lovers
To each other's arms?
What protects Olympus and unites the gods?
It is the spirit of man
　　　　　Expressed by the power
Of poetry,
　　　　　Won by poor sods

Like me,
Sweating over words
    Hour after hour.

ACTOR   Use it then,
                    This fabulous power,
             Like in a love affair: seduce
                    Us, lose
             Yourself in pain and ecstasy,
                    Throw away
             All restraint.
             Forget the middle-aged, pathetic
                    Nitpicking academic;
             Write
                    A text
             Full of fantasy,
                    With the ugly and the pretty,
             The serious and the silly,
                    Hand in hand.
             The old saying's true:
                    Love your audience
             And they'll love you.

POET   Oh, to sing
                    Like that,
             Give me back
                    The time when I began;
             When the songs sang
                    Themselves,
             Like water from a spring;
             Make me strong,
                    Raging with the pain
             Of love and hate,
             Make me young again.

ACTOR   Don't moan about age;
             Wonder and rage
                    Burn on,
             The wild-eyed
                    Child within you
             Never died.

DIRECTOR   Right. Stop navel gazing.
                    Time to try something amazing.

With all the theatre's tricks,
The whole mix:
The serious and the daft,
            The sun, the moon, the stars
Animals, rocks, plants;
For it is our ambition
            To use our craft
To pace out the circle of creation.
We have a story to tell:
            A little stroll
From heaven
            Through the world,
And all the way
            Down to hell.

2. Prologue in Heaven

The LORD, *the* HEAVENLY HOSTS. *Afterwards* MEPHIS-
TOPHELES. *The three* ARCHANGELS *come forward.*

RAPHAEL   The sun sings its old song,
                            A furnace thundering
                 Dawn to night
                            Across the sky,
                            Drowning the music of the spheres;
                 Angels draw strength
                 From the blazing light,
                 Though no angel can fathom
                            The mystery of the mechanism
                 Of high heaven.

GABRIEL   And planet Earth speeds in space,
                 Spinning its double face;
                 Bright paradise of day concedes
                            To hell of night;
                 And eternity's symphony,
                 The music of the spheres, fits
                            In counterpointed harmony:
                 The sea roars
                 And deep tides rip
                            The rocks of ocean floors
                 To bits . . .

MICHAEL   . . . And storms roll
                 Hand in hand, gripping the planet
                 Equator to pole;
                 Lightning flashes devastation
                         Sky to land
                 Before the thunderclap.
                 But, Oh Lord, you hold
                 The terrors of creation
                         Calmly in your hand;
                 Your angels kneel in adoration
                 As you walk, gently,
                         Along the paths of Heaven.

ALL THREE   No one, oh Lord, can know your ways:
                         Why the sky
                 Shines as bright as on the day you made it.
                         We are only fit to kneel in praise
                 As you pass by.

MEPH.   I see you are not too bored
                         To come out to see us again,
                 My Lord.
                 And here you find me,
                         Standing humbly
                 With the household servants.
                 I can't, I fear,
                         Be flowery
                 With words of praise,
                 Like the heavenly circle here;
                         After
                 Such solemnity, I would try to raise
                         A laugh,
                 But I know you've given up laughter.
                 I, myself, know little
                         Of the music of the spheres;
                 I work down on earth:
                 I just see how people slog away
                         Weighed down by their fears.
                 The little gods of that world seem
                 As weird as they were on the day
                         That you gave them birth;
                 They suffer so much pain
                 Because you put a gleam
                         Of heaven's light,

In the dim night
>Of the human brain;
They call it 'reason' and only use it
>To be more bestial than the beasts:
Humanity's song
>Is the buzz of a filthy fly,
Sung
>As it feasts
On dung.

LORD

You love the filth, you love to abuse
Mankind and accuse
His maker. Is there nothing good on earth?

MEPH.

Absolutely nothing at all:
>Gloom and doom, valleys of sorrows,
Bad todays and worse tomorrows.
Poor men and women, poor
>would-be gods;
What's the pleasure torturing
>The miserable sods?

LORD

I have always meant
>To lead humanity
To enlightenment.
Do you know Faust?

MEPH.

>The scientist philosopher?

LORD

My faithful servant.

MEPH.

He serves you very strangely.
Faust eats and drinks nothing real;
>The alcohol of fantasy
Makes him only half aware
>Of what is really there;
He wants to steal
>The brightest star
From heaven, yet wallow down below
>In all the pleasures of the earth.
He tears himself apart;
Nothing high or low, near or far,
>Can still
The violence of his troubled heart.

LORD   He worships me
                Despite his great confusion;
                All things are planned
                        And move to their conclusion.
                I will lead
                        Faust to salvation;
                The gardener will mend,
                With time, the damaged shoot;
                        The green young tree
                Will blossom in the end.

MEPH.   And yet,
                        My Lord,
                Perhaps a little bet?
                        With your permission,
                I'll lead him, gently,
                        To perdition.

LORD   I concur.
                As long as he lives, do your worst.
                To err
                        Is human in the human struggle.

MEPH.   I thank you.
                        It is tedious, torturing the ranks
                Of the dead; one longs
                        To get the tongs
                Into something fresh:
                The rosy cheeks of living flesh.
                I have the cat's know-how;
                        Mouse, I'm coming now.

LORD   Very well then,
                        I leave you to your game.
                Turn that soul from the light,
                Lead him to infernal night
                        If you can; then stand in shame,
                All your powers useless
                Against a good man
                        Who knows wrong from right.

MEPH.   I know
                        The bet is won
                Before I have begun;

                    I must crow
            Just a little, I will have
                    What I desire:
            Faust will breathe the burning dust
                    Of hell-fire.

LORD   You think you are free
                To harm, but you are harmless;
                        How could God hate
                The jester oblivious of his fate?

                Heaven closes. The ARCHANGELS *leave.*

MEPH.   (*Alone.*)
                Yes, now and then I look the old boy up,
                        To keep relations on a civil level;
                And it's very courteous of God, to sup
                        With me at all: I mean, I am the
                                                    Devil.

3. Night

A narrow, vaulted, gothic room: FAUST *sitting restlessly at his desk.*

FAUST   Years and years spent on philosophy,
                        Law, medicine,
                And, oh, tedium, theology:
                Years of dedicated drudgery,
                And for what?
                I'm as ignorant
                        As when I began;
                How can
                        I call myself master
                Of science and humanities?
                All my studies
                        Have ended in disaster:
                My learning is a pose,
                Ten years I've led
                        My wretched students by the nose.
                All I know is that we know
                Nothing, and it burns
                        My heart.

But why? Why? I'm not torn apart
By moral scruples, I'm free
      Of fear of the devil and hellfire.
And yet
I've had all the joy, all the desire
      Torn out of me;
I've failed to learn,
      How can I teach?
Who am I to reach
Out to others and preach
      Morality?
And I'm broke:
      No money, no property,
No honorary
      Doctorates,
No glittering prizes;
The long slog
      Of the struggle to learn
Is worse than the life of a dog.
So:
      So:
And so I turn to magic.
I yield to the powers of the spirit world.
I yearn to see unfurled
      All the hidden mysteries:
How the core of the earth
      Turns on its axis,
How the sun burns
      But keeps its course.
Magic will liberate me
      I'll no longer be
Enslaved by arid orthodoxy
      From academic books on a dusty
                  shelf:
      I will understand
The creative force of life itself.
So:
      So:
         Full moon,
Shine down
One more time upon my agony;
So many nights, my gloomy friend,
      I've sat here
Waiting for you to appear
      And throw your dim blue light

On the pages of my books.
Oh to walk out at night
In your lovely light;
      To fly over mountains,
Skim over fields; flow
      Through caves with spirits
In your glow,
Free of the sludge of knowledge
      That clogs and inhibits
The brain and the senses.
Oh to cleanse myself,
      To be born anew,
With your mystic light
Falling on my skin like dew.
But no:
      No:
Still blocked.
      Locked
In this hole, walled up
With rotting books,
      Their spines peeling;
Notes and smoke-brown papers
      Piled up to the ceiling;
The junk of years of study,
Jars of specimens gone cloudy,
Instruments long out of date.
Scholar,
      This intellectual squalor
Is your fate,
You're half dead:
      Your spirit dulls.
God made you to be free;
Instead
      You're shut up here
Amongst old bones and skulls,
      Smoke and decay.
Escape!
      Escape!
Fly away.
Of all the books you only need this one.
Magic book, you will be my guide
To the orbits of the stars, the wide
      Splendours of nature;
No more boring hours
Of logical thinking, scientific experimenting.

Now the whole
Universe will open for me, with this book
Spirits will speak to me,
I will set free the hidden powers
Of my soul.
Spirits, I feel you near,
Can you hear
Me?

*He opens the book and sees the sign of the
Macrocosmos.*

Pleasure melts my veins, bliss
Floods my senses at the sight of this,
The mighty sign of macrocosmos.
Was it a god who drew
These signs that still
My torment, that fill
My heart with joy,
The magic signs that drive
Nature's powers
And all that is alive?
Am I a god? An immortal light shines
In me;
I look at these designs and see
Nature bow
Before my soul. Now
I understand what the old magician said:
'The spirit world is open
It is you who are shut:
Up, acolyte, cut
Down fear, be reborn
Bathe naked in the magic of the dawn.'

He is looking at the sign.

What a spectacle, but
Only that. A pretty pattern.
How can I batten
On you, nature,
Grip you,
Fix me hard to you,
And suck you,
Suckle on the breast

Where heaven and earth
          Feed, and lie at rest . . .
Oh the need that flows,
          The pain that grows in vain . . .

*He turns the page angrily and sees the sign of
the spirit of Earth.*

The sign of the spirit of Earth.
Spirit, I feel my strength grow
          Within me,
Like the fiery glow
          Of new wine.
Suddenly I am alive
          With the courage
To survive
          All catastrophe;
To journey to the edge
          Of earth's extremes
Of pain and pleasure.
The clouds close;
          The light of the moon
Is hidden;
          The pressure
Lowers in the glass,
          The lamp glows
Dim;
Something forbidden
          Is about to come to pass . . .
A hissing haze of steam
          fills my brain,
Red rays
          Flash behind my eyes;
I feel it:
          A tremor, a sudden shudder
Deep in the cellars of the earth.
I feel you, Spirit:
          Show yourself to me!
You must, you must . . .
My senses reel . . .
Tear my mind and heart to bits,
Take my sanity, my health,
          Grind my flesh into the dust
But show yourself.

He takes the book and pronounces the sign of the Spirit mysteriously. A red flame flashes up, the Spirit appears in the flame.

SPIRIT   Who calls?

FAUST   Oh horror falls
        Upon my soul.

SPIRIT   You pulled me here,
        You wrenched me
From my sphere
Into your reality.

FAUST   I cannot bear to look at you.

SPIRIT   Are you the arrogant superman
Who thinks he can
        Instruct the spirits to appear?
Where is the true
        Faust, brave enough to do a deed
Of magic
        Calling to me in his need?
I came in pity for your passion,
But look at you:
        One breath from me
And you writhe in fear
        Like a worm.

FAUST   No. No. I'll not squirm
        Before a mere spectre;
I am Faust. I am as great as you.

SPIRIT   I fly to and fro
        To and fro,
Circling the globe,
As I work the roaring loom
        Of time;
My threads are the threads of life
The wave
        Of the eternal sea,
The womb,
        The grave;
With them I weave
        Nature's living robe.

FAUST   Oh great spirit, my brother
                          Weaver of nature's secrets,
                 We are like each other.

SPIRIT   No. You are like another.
                          Not me.

The SPIRIT OF EARTH *disappears.*

FAUST   (*Collapsing.*)
                 Not you? You mean I
                          Am made in the image of my creator?
                 Or do you mean . . . I am like an even greater
                          Spirit?
                 Who is it? Am I . . .
                 (*Whisper.*) As great as God?

A knock on the door.

FAUST   Oh no. My student. The clod
                          Hopper bore
                 Wagner, knocking on my door;
                 And there will be no reason, no reason,
                          Only to bore me the more.

WAGNER *in dressing gown and nightcap, a
lamp in his hand.* FAUST *turns to him, angrily.*

WAGNER   Were you reading Greek?
                 Greek is full of tragic passions.
                 I had to have a peek. Could Greek be a factor
                 In getting good marks? Will you give me
                                                lessons?
                 'Let the priest learn from the actor',
                 That's the saying.

FAUST   A good priest is an actor:
                          Preaching and praying
                 Is theatrical faking.

WAGNER   I've been studying all day.
                 It's like looking down binoculars the wrong way.

If trying hard, if sweat of the brow
Counted, I'd be a genius by now.

FAUST   Instinct; go with the heart,
                         If you don't feel it
                 Forget it.

WAGNER   But the orator succeeds by hammering out a
                                                    style;
                 Sweat and hard labour, the midnight oil;
                 Knowledge is like bricks built up in a pile;
                 It's ceaseless work and honest toil.

FAUST   Reason is effortless,
                         Great art, artless;
                 If you have something true to say
                 The words will come.
                 Go away, scrape a crumb
                 From an honest living;
                         Forget this rhetorical rot,
                 Words rattling
                         Like dead leaves:
                 You've either got the talent
                         Or you've not.

WAGNER   Ars longa vita brevis;
                 My thoughts jam in paralysis,
                 My head and heart are stuffed with pain.
                 I descend into philosophy's deep pothole,
                 Intellectual crampons on my brain.
                 Many have tried the descent and died.
                 But what pleasure is the treasure
                 Of history, to travel to the past and unravel
                 The wisest thoughts of the wisest men;
                 To see how we came here from where we
                                                    were then.

FAUST   My dear, dear, pathetic friend,
                 The past is a locked junk room:
                         No one can go in.
                 No, the past
                         Is a rubbish-bin;
                 No, the past
                         Is a tatty puppet play.

The lessons of history?
        Banalities,
Only fit for puppets to say.

WAGNER   But the workings of the heart and mind, the
                                    grand
Scheme of the world; if only we could
                              understand
A bit of what it's about.

FAUST   Understand?
                You'll get your hand
Cut off, tongue cut out;
It's the stake for the few
        Who understand.
But please, my friend,
        May we end this . . .
Profound peregrination?
I have a deep fascination
        For everything you say,
But I need my sleep.

WAGNER   My dear Faust, you're right.
Day or night,
My enthusiasms
Tend to come in spasms.
But tomorrow is Good Friday;
Give me something of the holy day
To discuss with me; my studies bring
Me some insights, but I want to know
        Everything.

WAGNER *exits*.

FAUST   A fool with a mind like glue
That squirms,
        Stuck to the second rate:
He wants to dig up treasures
        And is happy with worms.
No wait.
        This thick ape
Of a student
Was my escape;
The sight of the spirit

Struck me with terror.
I was face to face
With insanity.
Oh mighty force
What was my error?
I conjured you
But could not hold you to me.
Oh ecstasy,
For a second
I was at once
Gigantic as the world
And small as a molecule;
The power of a god
beckoned.
But you were cruel:
You crushed me,
Back into this miserable shape,
This clod
Of earth called man.
Who will teach me the magic?
I am made of dust and dead matter;
I am the worm
That picnickers flick
From the table cloth.
I am dust, dead matter and muck;
The moth
Chomps into the world
Of dust, dead matter and muck;
Books, furniture, possessions, the junk
Of daily life
Have buried me; I am curled
Up underground, sunk
In dust, dead matter and muck . . .
How we torture ourselves over the centuries,
Dreaming of forbidden things
That will help our escape from this:
That mankind the worm is a chrysalis,
That we will grow immortal wings.
What are you grinning at, skull?
Your brain, once, struggled with hope and
passion
Toward the light, only to disintegrate
In the dull
Dusk of confusion.
And the worn out instruments

Of failed experiments,
My father's old apparatus,
Do you reproach me too?
Oh to crash
Through the tedium, to tear
Up years of failed research
In a flash;
By one act, in one
Mad moment TO KNOW.
That phial.
Why do I stare
At that phial?
The poison I made,
Why does it glow
Like the moon in a dark forest?
Tiny phial I worship you,
I lift you in reverence;
You
Are all of man's intelligence
In a little glass;
Pass
To me your powers,
Have pity on me . . .
Already in my mind
I see
A chariot of fire
To take me
To the spheres . . .
Yes, I'll turn
My back against the sun.
What if I burn?
I have no fears,
I'll rip open
The gates
Of death;
Gods, spirits, fates,
Man in his dignity
Is as brave as you.
Now I will go down
Into the dark cave
Where the imagination
Condemns itself
To its own damnation;
Happily I go
On the dangerous journey,

Around the blazing
Mouth of hell;
I risk everything
Sanity and health
My life itself.
Is Faust to fall
Into nothingness?
Yes. Cheerfully.
He couldn't care less.
Down. Time to raise
A glass:
I toast my last breath
In the sun's first rays.

*He takes the chalice to his lips. There is a
sound of church bells and a CHOIR singing.*

CHOIR OF ANGELS

Christ the Lord is risen
Man's great sin
Will be forgiven;
God rejoices
In high heaven,
Christ the Lord is risen.

FAUST

What sound
Rings
On the rim of the glass,
Pushing it from my lips?
Is it heaven that sings
To me,
That will not let me pass
From this world?
What was I about to do?
Was I striving
To reach the spheres above
By the horror of suicide?
The simple joy
Of simple faith in heaven's love
Died long ago in me.
Yet . . . I have a memory . . . when I was a
boy . . .

The choir singing,
My childlike faith
Shining on Easter morning.

Sing on, ring on heavenly sound;
    My tears fall,
I am a man of no worth.
A memory of childhood innocence
Brings me back to earth.

4. Outside the Gates

All sorts of people are going for a walk.

FIRST STUDENT
    Here come the servant girls;
    It's strong beer and blonde curls
    For me.

CITIZEN'S DAUGHTER
    What a pity.
    See those students ?
        Good looks and all the luck
    In the world,
    Running after common muck.

SECOND STUDENT (*To the* FIRST.)
    Hey, those two.
    The one on the right's my neighbour's
                daughter.
    My type: black hair, eyes of blue.

FIRST STUDENT
    The kind of girl who knows she didn't oughta
        Talk to the likes of you.
    Never touch the bourgeoisie!
        Come on,
    It's the pub and servant girls for me:
    All the beer that you can drink,
    Then the charm of arms grown strong
        Scrubbing at the sink.

CITIZEN   But what has this new mayor
    Done for the city? One could despair:
        Things get worse and worse,
    Standards are too lax.
    And as for the level of tax . . .

BEGGAR   (*Singing.*)
                        Please be kind, kind sir
                                A coin from your pocket;
                        If your heart is hard,
                        Please unlock it.
                        Pretty lady, please,
                                In your Easter dress;
                        Giving wins God's gift
                                Of happiness.

ANOTHER CITIZEN
                        It's a definition of civilisation,
                        To walk in the park on a Sunday
                        And talk of far away atrocities:
                        The human tragedies
                                Of foreign wars.
                        To be civilised is to be born, well . . . here,
                                And nowhere near
                        The Balkans, Russia, Eastern Turkey.
                        Drink in hand, one counts oneself lucky,
                        As one stands on one's veranda, looking down
                                At our native land,
                        So prosperous and happy.

THIRD CITIZEN I say stay out of a foreign war,
                        Just slam the door
                                Shut;
                        Let the animals cut
                                'Emselves to bits.

OLD WOMAN   (*To* CITIZEN'S DAUGHTERS.)
                        Pretty thing, hot blood
                        Pounding under your pretty dress,
                        You're in luck;
                                Shall I bring
                        What you burn to possess?
                        A young buck officer out for stud?

THE OTHER WOMAN
                        She showed me my lover
                        In a crystal ball,
                                Handsome, arrogant and tall;
                        Then I saw him pass
                        Into a cloud inside the glass.

I looked everywhere;
He'd disappeared
Into thin air.

SOLDIERS   Mighty castles with high walls,
Pretty girls with mocking eyes;
Girls and castles must surrender,
The boldest soldier wins the prize.

FAUST *and* WAGNER.

FAUST   Spring sets free the frozen river,
Feeble old winter
Flees to the mountains;
Weakened, he scatters down light
Frost upon the fields;
But the sun hates cold and white;
The monochrome of winter yields
To brilliant colour.
I know that on this hill
There are no flowers, but look down there:
Crowds in their Sunday best spill
From the city gates into the country;
The sun has used its powers
To open huge blooms of humanity
Right across the valley.
Easter, the resurrection;
But people too have risen
From narrow streets,
From damp unhealthy rooms,
From the tombs
They're buried in in daily life:
Worry, work, family strife,
The scraping for money.
Listen: the villages are humming
With music and laughter and dancing.
Yes, this is my land
Of milk and honey;
I say get out of the shadow
Of church and steeple,
Celebrate the rebirth
Of the hopes of the common people;
I want my heaven on earth.

WAGNER   I treasure the pleasure of a walk and a talk
              With you, Herr Doctor, but I fear
              These thugs and their women hate us.
                      Even to hear
              Their devil's music on coarse fiddles,
              The shouts of louts playing skittles,
                      Dangerously belittles
              One's status;
              Popular culture of this kind
              Seriously rots the mind.

OLD PEASANT   Doctor Faust,
              You are a scholar and a gentleman;
              It's wonderful that you find
              Time to come out here.
              Please sir,
                      Drink a beer
              On us; your father
              Saved many from the fever
                      In the epidemic;
              You too were in and out
                      The houses of the sick,
              Trying your best
                      Even when they died.
              You passed a terrible test,
              Though you were just a boy.
              So health 'n' joy
                      To you, doctor!

ALL   Health to the good doctor
              Protector of the poor!

FAUST   Good friends, we all are patients,
              Kneeling at heaven's door.

              FAUST *and* WAGNER *go on.*

WAGNER   You must feel very proud
              To be worshipped by the crowd.

FAUST   Let's make for that rock,
                      And rest.
              During the fever
                      I'd sit here, alone,

In agony,
          In panic,
Shouting 'Why? Why?',
Raging at the Lord of the sky
          To end the epidemic.
Applause of the crowd?
          For the heroic
Father and son?
          Mockery.
We were quacks.
          Our cures?
All fraud, fakery.
My father was a gloomy
          Man, a dark eminence,
A dabbler in alchemy
Shut in his alchemical kitchen, mixing
          Opposite to opposite,
The endless magical
          recipes.
All through these mountains
          And valleys,
Famous father and saintly son
          Poisoned thousands.

WAGNER   But what can a decent man do?
            All you did was practise conscientiously
            The arts that you believed to be true.

FAUST   No. We knew what we had done.
            Happy the man free of the terror
                      Of drowning in a sea of error.
            Sometimes I fear
            That what we need to know we never will;
            And what we *do* know, we can only use to kill.
            The sun lowers;
                      The day begins to die,
            The hollow
                      Valley darkens.
            If only I could follow,
                      Fly
            After the sun
                      In everlasting evening light;
            Glide in flight
            Above the beautiful world,

                    Mountains and valleys unfurled
                    Beneath me,
                              Until I circled
                    The globe
                    Over deserts, continents, the oceans.

WAGNER   Yes, I've had fanciful notions
                    Though nothing quite as fancy as flight.
                    Personally, I get fed up with grandeur:
                    Mountains, the lurid effects of nature.
                    I'm much happier
                              Tucked up on a winter's night;
                    I need to look no further than the pages of
                                                            a book
                    To see mountain ranges; the sea
                    Of ideas is enough for me.

FAUST   My dear Wagner,
                              You're lucky
                    You only know one way of thinking;
                    May you never discover
                              Its opposite.
                    Two souls live within me,
                              They cling to each other:
                    One burns
                              With the coarse desires of the world,
                    The other yearns
                              To rise to the realms of light.
                    I dream of flight to a new life:
                    Spirits of the air,
                              If you are there,
                    Halfway between heaven and earth,
                    Take me away.

WAGNER   This is foolish and dangerous. Never pray
                    To the hordes that hover in the ether;
                    They pretend to be from heaven but they lie;
                    Have truck with them and your very soul
                                                        could die.
                    But it's getting cold, let's go home.
                    Feet up and a cup of something warm;
                    There's fog in the air.
                              What's the matter?

FAUST   That black dog there
                        Running in that field.

WAGNER   It's a dog.

FAUST   Running through the grass in circles.

WAGNER   Just a dog.

FAUST   A mad motion,
                        Round and round in spirals;
                It's hunting us.

WAGNER   An optical illusion.

FAUST   Nearer and nearer,
                        The circles tightening!

WAGNER   There's nothing frightening;
                        It's a dog not a ghost.

FAUST   Boy, come here, boy!

WAGNER   A poodle. A stupid breed;
                        More a toy
                Than a dog.

FAUST   You're right. It's just a stupid animal,
                Nothing supernatural.

WAGNER   It's pointless complaining
                About a dog's behaviour;
                Discipline's the saviour:
                As with men it's all a matter of training.

5. Faust's Study

FAUST *entering with the poodle.*

FAUST   I leave the fields where,
                Beneath the cover,
                Of night holy terrors hover.

Now
Wild whirring thoughts no longer tear
At my mind;
I feel the slow stirring
Of a love of God and mankind.

The friendly lamp burns
In my tiny study;
Now my heart is ready
For the light again; reason returns,
Hope revives;
        Days will be as bright
As they were in the spring of our lives.

What was that thought? No.
No that's not right.
My thoughts can't stay on heaven
When my dog growls down below.
Shut up dog!
        I want the singing
Of angels around me,
Not the whining
        Of a poodle.
Ignorant people
        Sneer and spit at beauty and art:
Do poodles too?
        Is this the whine
Of a canine philistine?
No matter.
        It's gone.
Sublime thoughts shatter.
But I can still
Drink to my fill
        At the source
Of spiritual contentment.
Turn it, turn it open,
The New Testament and . . .
St John's gospel
        First line:
'In the beginning was the word.'
        Word? No. That ought
To be:
'In the beginning was thought.'
        No. Now I see it clearly.
'In the beginning was energy.'

No. Now The holy spirit
Is helping me:
          Quick!
Let the first line of the gospel read:
'In the beginning was THE DEED.'

Poodle, be
          Quiet;
If you go on howling and barking,
One of us will have to leave the room,
          And I'm afraid
It won't be me.

Dog . . . ?
          What's happening?
My poodle's stretching,
          A terrible power
Is changing his body;
          Grotesque!
That's not the shape of a dog,
          That's a hippopotamus,
And, beneath
          The hippo's lip,
Terrifying, gnashing teeth . . .
Can't hell
          Do any more
Than you?
This will see you off;
          The Spell Of Four.

          Salamander shall glow;
          Undine shall boil;
          Sylph shall slow;
          Kobold shall toil.

          Salamander
                    Vanish in a fiery haze;
          Undine
                    Blaze,
          Be the flash of a meteor in the sky;
          Sylph,
                    Be my
          Home spirit, my friend;
          Kobold, incubus,
          Bring all to an end!

Oh. No effect.
He just lies there and grins.

Are you a fugitive?
   Are your sins
So great, no spell
   Can blow you back down to hell?
Then look upon this sign,
   Before which
All Devils fall to their knees,
   And hell itself must freeze . . .
It's changing,
Bristly hair growing;
It's swelling
It's dissolving,
   Into a mist;
It's filling
   The room . . .
Bad boy, bad dog,
I'll burn you I'll damn you,
   Shoo!
I can incant
   A dog's doom:
You'll whine, you'll pant,
   Your claws
Will fall from your paws,
Your fur will catch fire,
   A hot wire
Will tear off your tail.
   My magic cannot fail:
Shoo. Shoo.
   Don't bite me, don't bite me . . .

MEPHISTOPHELES *comes forward from
behind the stove as the mist disperses, dressed
like a travelling scholar.*

MEPH.   Why the row?
      Relax;
   I'm in your service now.

FAUST   *You* broke
      Out of the poodle's fur?
   Is this a joke?

MEPH.   Not for me, dear sir:
                        Your magical technique
             Really made the pips squeak.

FAUST   What is your name?

MEPH.   Do you care?
                        What's the sense
             Of such a trivial question
             From such a famous scholar,
                        Who's always either up in the air
             With thoughts of the sublime,
             Or in the depths of despair,
             Looking for essence
                        In the primeval slime?

FAUST   The name of your kind
                        Is a charm,
             It reveals the harm
                        Of an evil mind.
             Example:
                        Lord Of The Flies;
             Destroyer;
                        Beelzebub The Liar;
             Lord Of The Middle Air.
             So, who are you?

MEPH.   I am a part of that power
                        That longs to do evil,
             But ends up doing good.

*& opposite
p. 25*

FAUST   A riddle?
                        How could evil
             Ever do good?

MEPH.   I negate.
                        Why?
             Because all that is born
                        Is only fit to die;
             All being is
                        Best as nothingness.
             My job? Let's say I'm in
             Creative cosmic negativity;
                        Or 'Sin'.

FAUST I don't understand.
You said you were part of a power,
  But you stand
There whole.

MEPH. Is 'wholeness' all?
  Humanity
Is a little world of fools
  That thinks it's whole;
I, in contrast, am a model of modesty:
  I know I am part of a part
Of the darkness,
The great nothing
`   That, at the moment of creation,
Gave birth to light;
Hated light, blazing in celebration
  Of victory over Mother Night.
But I give you a paradox:
  For light to blaze
Matter must burn
  And die;
Matter blocks
  The eternal life of light.
Soon
  Both matter and light will die;
The universe will darken
And the kingdom of night return.

FAUST But is it because you fail
To destroy on the cosmic scale,
That you bother to appear
  To the likes of me?

MEPH. Yes, it's agreeably nasty,
  But all pretty petty these days.
This crude, stupid world,
  This bungled creation
Is always finding ways
  To avoid destruction.
I throw the lot at them:
Floods, storms, earthquakes,
Public riot, domestic mayhem;
  Here a famine, there a civil war.
I ruin, I torture, I blind

But that damn animal, humankind,
       Punch-drunk, battered,
Dim, spattered
       With blood,
Keeps coming back for more.
It drives me crazy: this filthy
       Muck, this stuff
From which they're made
       Seethes with new life;
Thousands of seeds
Sow new generations,
       And I
Have to wipe out millions
All over again;
       When will they cry
'Enough's enough'?

FAUST

So,
Against the eternally active, creative spirit
All you can do is spit.
Poor son of Chaos,
       Your hate and malice are at a loss:
You should give something else a try.

MEPH.

I'm working on the odd idea.
       But just for now
Will you let me out of here?

FAUST

Surely you're free
       To come and go?
Be my guest: fly up the chimney,
Go through the wall;
Or, more boringly,
       Just walk out the door.

MEPH.

This is embarrassing.
       It's the pentagram on the floor.

FAUST

The spell
       Has trapped you?
But you got here from hell,
       Why can't you go back?

MEPH.   The lack
                      Of a point: that angle
             Is not joined;
                      Evil needs precision.

FAUST   So, by accident,
             I built the Devil a prison.

MEPH.   The poodle didn't look.
                      This is tricky . . .

FAUST   Avoid the sign.
                      Rise in the air, go
             Out of the window.

MEPH.   No no.
                      Devils and ghosts
             Must do things by the book.
                      The regulation is exact:
             Exit by the means of entry.

FAUST   You mean
                      Even hell has laws?
             I could make a contract
             With you gentlemen
                      That you could never break?

MEPH.   A signed, sealed, guaranteed, legally bound,
             Sealed, delivered, all above ground
             One hundred percent water-proof deal;
                      And not a legal fee to pay.
             But, for the moment,
                      Could you see your way
             To let me . . . ?

FAUST   I'm afraid not. This is unique.
             I've made a fool
                      Of the Devil;
             The Lord Of Misrule
                      Is trapped
             'Cos he can't break a rule!

MEPH.   Oh all right.
             I'll while away a little time;

                    Perhaps with a few tricks,
          To show you something of my style?

FAUST   A devil's magic show?

MEPH.   My friend,
                    Prepare
               For pleasure beyond measure.
               The spirits
               Will seduce
                    You away
               From reality,
                    You will bathe
               In the juice
                    Of sensuality,
               Smell, taste,
                    Touch,
               Sight,
                    Hearing
               Heightened
                    So much,
               That your flesh itself
                    Will sing.
               This is true sorcery:
                    The lifting
               Of the senses
                    To ecstasy.
               Let us begin!

THE SPIRITS   Vanish arches
                     Of the night,
                     Patches
                     Of dark cloud;
                     Blaze light
                     Of rising suns:
                     The celestial ones,
                     The children
                     Of heaven,
                     Are floating past
                     Glittering
                     Among the stars.
                     Desire follows
                     The fluttering ribbons
                     Of their clothes,

As they pass
Over flowery hollows
Where lovers lie,
Giving themselves
To each other
Forever in the grass.
Couple after couple,
Bower after bower,
Gleaming
Limbs, tangled
Tight in tendrils
Of love and dreams.
Wine spills in streams
Sparkling over precious stones
Down mountains
Into glowing lakes;
Birds drink and fly away
To bright islands far
Beyond night, beyond day,
Where the sons of heaven race
Across the lakes, run
In the high mountains,
Fly into the air,
Searching for the distant star
Of happiness and grace.

MEPH. He's asleep.
Spirits, I am deeply
  In your debt.
Now, sad man, did you think
  You can shrink
The Devil into a beetle in a bottle?
I am caught up a bit here, though. How . . .
Yes. I need the tooth of a rat.
'The Lord of rats 'n' mice
Of Frogs 'n' bug 'n' lice
Conjures' . . . Ah. Hello rat.
  Bite that
Angle of the pentagram. Well done.
Back to your hole.
Faust, be happy in your dream
  For now,
As my great scheme
  Tightens round your soul.

FAUST   (*Waking up*.)
                 Dream? Am I ill?
                 Was that poodle
                 A grotesque hallucination?
                 I'm too old to enjoy a children's game
                         Of making friends with the Devil;
                 But too young not to feel
                         How wonderful it would be
                 If the illusion were real.
                 For what has the world to offer me?
                 'Sacrifice, sacrifice
                         Suppress all vice;'
                 That's the world's life-long song.
                 I wake in the morning
                         In terror;
                 The day picks
                         On every little error,
                 Kicks
                         At every little twinge
                 Of pleasure;
                 All the instincts
                         Of my heart
                 Cringe; come the night
                         Anxiety
                 Covers my bed; I cower
                         In fright
                 At what the dreams may bring.
                 The god in my heart
                         Rules by instinct and passion;
                 The god in my head
                         Can only understand with reason.
                 My existence is a burden:
                         I wish that I were dead.

6. Faust's Study

FAUST *and* MEPHISTOPHELES. *A knock on the door.*

FAUST   Come in.

MEPH.   It's me.

FAUST   Right. Come in.

MEPH.   You've got to say it three times.
                    Do you mind?

FAUST   Come in.

MEPH.   Too kind.
               Why the scholarly gloom?
               You spend too much time
                    Alone in this room.
               See I'm come to cheer you up a bit,
               Dressed as an aristocratic idiot.
               This is the gear only Lords can afford:
               The red gold trim,
                    Silk coat,
               Feather on the hat rim,
               Fashionable state-of-the-art
                    Sword.
               Quick, get kitted up too;
               Wearing this we can float
                    Through society and do
               Anything we want to do.

FAUST   Clothes are just the same as human skin
               Only fit for dying in.

MEPH.   But death's not a thing you
               Dream of slipping into.

FAUST   I do.
                    Happy the man
               Wrapped in death's bloodstained cloak;
                    Better to take the chance
               And get cut to bits in a war,
               Or croak
                    In a girl's bed,
               Or just drop dead
                    At a dance.
               Oh to drop, lifeless as a stone,
               Before the heavenly throne.

MEPH.   And who,
               The other night, had the wherewithal
               To do it –
                    A little phial of brown juice –
               And wouldn't use it?

FAUST   Does spying
                        Excite you?
             Is there nowhere to hide?

MEPH.   I do not omnisciently know it all
             But I cast
                        My network wide:
             My information is vast.

FAUST   What matters what is known or unknown?
             All knowledge is illusion;
             I curse the deception
                        Of wild dreams,
             Curse the attraction
                        Of possessions,
             Curse
                        Home, wife, child;
             I curse the great god Money,
                        Plumping fat cushions
             For idle pleasures;
             I curse all earthly,
                        I curse all heavenly
             Treasures;
             I curse all faith, I curse all hope.

SPIRITS   Yes, yes, curse
                        All that rancours
                        And angers you,
                        Weave a rope
                        Of all the world's wrongs
                        To hang it by;
                        Or
                                try
                        A new way,
                        A new life
                        Bright with hope,
                        Sensuality,
                        New songs,
                        New colours.

MEPH.   Yes, all this soulful
                        Wallowing and sorrowing,
             It's revolting:
             Do you want your life to be

                    Dead meat,
              Picked at by a vulture?
                    You need reviving,
              Convivial company;
              Even the worst examples of humanity
                    Must be more fun
              Than this lonely striving
                    For high culture.
              Bind your life with me,
              I will be faithful and I will be true;
                    Together we will go
              Everywhere, high and low;
              Though I'm not
                    One of the truly mighty
              Powers from below,
              I'll be your faithful shadow,
                    Your servant and your slave.

FAUST   What do I give away?

MEPH.   Discuss terms another day.

FAUST   No No.
              The Devil is an egoist.
              He does nothing for anybody
              Out of charity.
                    To hire him as a servant,
              That's really living dangerously.
              I insist:
                    State your conditions clearly!

MEPH.   I will enslave myself to you, I'll be
                    Bound fast
              To your command, all night, all day;
              Then, when you have passed
                    To the other side,
              You will do the same for me.

FAUST   'The other side' can wait;
              It's the here and now on earth
                    I love;
              This sky, this world, this sun
                    Shining above
              My pleasures and my sufferings.

When this world's smashed to bits
     The next one can have its turn.
I'll take my chance, I'll survive or burn.

MEPH.   That's the spirit. Do it.
               Bind yourself to me,
                    And up we'll fly, far away.
               You'll be dazzled at my tricks,
                    It'll be pleasure and kicks
               All the way:
                    See what
               No man has ever seen,
                    Go where
               No man has ever been.

FAUST   But, poor devil,
                    What could you ever
               Offer me?
               Your kind have never
                    Understood the grand
               Aspirations of humanity.
               All you have to give is food
                    That leaves you hungry,
               Gold that melts in the hand,
               A girl who lies in your arms
                    Dreaming of the man next door,
               The trappings of fame gone in a flash
                    Like a falling meteor.
               Show me fruit that rots away
                    Before it's picked;
               A tree that changes its leaves
                    Everyday.

MEPH.   No problem, easy.

FAUST   I'll agree
                    To this:
               If I grow lazy;
                    If I
               Ever believe your flattery,
               If you trap me
                    In depravity,
               You get
                    All of me.
               That's my bet.

MEPH.   Agreed.

FAUST   And if I ever
                       Want to freeze the fleeting
             Moment, saying
                       'You are too beautiful,
             Stay,'
                       Then chain me,
             Let me die;
                       My funeral bell
             Will tell you that you're free
             From my service;
                       Time will stop,
             The hour hand will drop
                       From the clock's face;
             My life will have run its race.

MEPH.   Morbid of you. And unwise.
                       Our contract ties
             You up. We won't forget.

FAUST   I don't care. I've not blasphemed.
                       All I've said
             Is that if I'm untrue to what I've always
                  dreamed,
             If I stagnate, I'm dead:
             Whether I'm your slave in hell or not
                       It doesn't matter.

MEPH.   Fine. Can we dot
             The odd i, cross the odd t?

FAUST   Won't my word do on its own?
                       I find words die
             The moment the pen
                       Touches the paper.
             Oh alright then.
                       Where
             Do you want me to write it?
             On parchment, metal, stone,
                       Water, sand, air . . .

MEPH.   Stop. Let this hysteria pass.
                       You only need a drop

Of blood,
          Scribbled on anything you've got.

FAUST   Sign in blood? Why not?
               It's all a farce.

MEPH.   Blood is a very special juice,
               A liquid for magical use.

FAUST   Don't be afraid, I'll not betray
                    Our agreement:
               I was arrogant, all
                    Self-aggrandizement,
               But now I know my place.
               I am no better than you.
               The eternal spirit turns away,
                    Nature hides her face;
               The thread of thought breaks,
               All knowledge nauseates;
               Now I will embrace
                    All that dissipates,
               Satisfy all appetites:
               Let's fly to the heights
                    Of passions,
               Dive to the depths
                    Of sensuality;
               Let's fall into the vortex
               Of time, the mystery
                    Of the cycle of history;
               Let pleasure and pain
                    Disaster and success
               Follow as they will,
                    All that matters
               Is human energy,
               To plunge into the process.

MEPH.   Indeed, there can never
                    Be an excess
               Of pleasure;
               I know you have exquisite taste,
               And while we are flying
                    If you fancy something,
               Don't let the opportunity
                    To indulge
               Go to waste.

FAUST   You don't understand me.
                              This has nothing
                 To do with indulgence.
                 I dedicate myself to frenzy;
                 My heart rejects
                              The intellectual life,
                 I embrace
                              The storm and stress
                 Of emotional strife;
                              The greatest excess
                 Of pain in pleasure,
                              The greatest excess
                 Of pleasure in pain.
                              I want to know
                 All the sorrow, all the happiness,
                              All the ills
                 We experience,
                 To go beyond the personal and the selfish:
                 I want my mind
                              To expand until it fills
                 With the totality
                              Of humankind:
                 My inner self will be all their selves
                 Until, like them, I perish.

MEPH.   Totality is a hopeless project.
                              We've been chewing totality
                 For thousands of years,
                 And it's stale bread, stale bread;
                 Unachievable by man or devil.
                 Believe me:
                              Don't bother.
                 The wholeness of reality
                              Is strictly for God.
                 He lives in eternal light,
                              We devils in eternal night;
                 As for your kind
                              You find
                 Wholeness is denied;
                 You are divided;
                              Both light and dark
                 Struggle inside of you.

FAUST   But I have free will.

I want to strike
A blow for humanity,
To become what we should be:
　　　godlike.

MEPH.　　　You are what you are.
　　　　　　　Bend
Your appearance,
Put a wig on your head,
　　　　Walk on high heels:
But it's all a dead end.
　　　　You will always be
What you are.

FAUST　　　Yes. The pointless vanity.
　　　　　　I piled up
All the treasures of the mind:
　　　　But now I sit here
Weak, blind
　　　　To any insight;
Not a hair's breadth
　　　　Nearer to infinity.

MEPH.　　　Unworthy of you, Doctor,
　　　　　　I fear
You are guilty here
　　　　Of conventional thinking:
You see, and don't
　　　　See, what most of your kind
See and don't.
But you've got legs, feet, hands, arms
　　　　Head, belly and arse:
Don't they give you
　　　　'Free will' enough?
Dump this philosophical stuff,
　　　　Plunge
Into the wide world's sea of charms;
The man who agonizes
　　　　Wins no prizes;
Devils lead him round and round
By a ring in his nose,
　　　　Like a dumb bull
Treading mud;
　　　　While nearby

Lie sweet meadows,
　　　　Lush with grass
For juicy chewing of the cud.

FAUST　　　　Alright. How do we go about
　　　　　　　Doing this?

MEPH.　　　　We just go. No
More nerve wracking, head cracking
Torture,
　　　　Tutoring the unteachable young;
It'll be
　　　　A relief to them as much as to you
When you're flung
　　　　To the ends of the earth,
To the ends of passion
　　　　On our great journey.
Go on, then. Get yourself ready.
　　　　Though do allow me
To get rid of those
　　　　Terrible clothes;
Travel and passion
Do require a certain sense of fashion.

Exit FAUST.

MEPH.　　　　I'll drag him through the banal brutality
The brutish banality
　　　　Of the lowest of life;
He'll wriggle, he'll writhe with lies
And when he's paralysed
　　　　I'll dangle little bits, tips
Of food to his lips;
He shall have the agony of insatiability;
He will beg, desperate for nourishment;
Even if he had no contractual obligation
He'd still end up on the Devil's plate,
Served up in a sauce
　　　　Of spiritual pain;
And so he will remain
　　　　In a state
Of delicious obliteration.

FAUST *enters. He carries a big suitcase.*

FAUST   Now what do we do?

MEPH.   The choice is yours.
                  I suggest
        We consult the menu.
                  For hors-d'oeuvres,
        Low life.
                  Second course,
        High life.
        Yes. Best get something
                  Tasty down you.

FAUST   Low life? I can't. It's useless.
        I become sick with shyness.
        I've been shut up in my study
                  For too long:
        I'll stand out, I just don't belong.

MEPH.   Don't panic
                  Confidence is a trick:
        Just give yourself a kick
                  And you've got it.
        Though, looking at you,
                  To tell the truth
        You could do
                  With a tonic:
        A sip of the elixir of youth.
        Good! Let's leave right now.

FAUST   But how . . .

MEPH.   Step one:
                  Stand on my coat.
        Step two:
                  Up in the air
        And off we float.
        No suitcase, no heavy packing;
        You will be lacking
                  Nothing, you'll be there
        In a split second, flying
        On a little breath of fiery air.
        Welcome to
                  Your new way of living.

7. Auerbach's Tavern in Leipzig

A drinking party.

BRANDER   (*Banging on the table.*)
Oi! Oi! What's wrong
     With the lot of yer?
A bit of hush all round!
     I thank you.
Now, seeing as we've got lovers
     Here tonight,
It's only right
To have a little love song.

He sings.

There was a little rat
He got very fat
     Living in the cellar;
Eating butter
He got fatter
     More than Martin Luther.
The cook put poison out
Ratty had to shout
     'I'm stuffed up like a lover'

CHORUS   (*Gleefully.*)
Stuffed up like a lover.

BRANDER   Onto the stove he ran
Into the frying pan
     Wheezy and falling over.
As he died
Ratty cried
     'Cook why do you bother?'
Came her cruel reply:
'I want to see you fry
     Stuffed up like a lover.'

CHORUS   Stuffed up like a lover.

SIEBEL   What a load of boring prats,
     Singing about rats.

BRANDER   Got
                       A soft spot
               For rats, then?

ALTMAYER   Look at that:
               The beer belly with the bald head,
               Sat in here to avoid the wife?
               So defeated by life
                       He thinks he *is* a swollen rat.

FROSCH   Doesn't anyone want
               To put a few beers away with style?
                       You're all sitting here steaming
               Like a pile of dung.

BRANDER   Don't whine.
                       What's been
               Your artistic contribution?
               What filthy song have you sung?

FROSCH   You want art? Here's art.

               FROSCH *pours the glass over his head.*

BRANDER   Stupid, stupid swine . . .

SIEBEL   Pull 'em apart!
                       No more or you two, you're out.
               Come on, lungs full. Give it a shout:
                       Ooh la ooh la, ooh la ooh la . . . (etc.)

ALTMAYER   Help! This bloke's bust my eardrums.

SIEBEL   Great big bums
                       Support great big voices
               And all of heaven rejoices.

FROSCH   Right. If you don't like it
                       Shut up and get out.

ALTMAYER   Tara tara, ooh ta ooh ta . . .

FROSCH   A tune, a tune, here it comes:

(*Sings.*)

> The dear old Holy Empire,
> Rotting wood
>> Only good
> For putting on a bonfire . . .

BRANDER   Political song,
>> Boring boring;
> Thank God every morning
>> I don't wake up and find
> I'm the Holy Roman Emperor.
> Politicians? Give 'em all a rope
>> To hang 'emselves;
> I know what:
> Let's elect a really strong
>> Leader,
> Let's elect a Pope.

FROSCH   (*Sings.*)
> Soar on frail
>> Wing,
> Nightingale;
>> Sing
> Of me and greet
>> My sweet
> Abigail.

SIEBEL   No soppy
>> Love songs,
> Or I'll really
>> Cut up stroppy.

Enter FAUST *and* MEPHISTOPHELES.

MEPH.   Let me initiate you to the joys
>> Of drunken company,
> A night out with the boys;
>> Senseless with happiness
> And wine and ale
> Their heads spin
>> Like a kitten chasing its tail.
> And, as long as the hangover's
>> Not life threatening,

                     And the landlord's running a slate,
                             Next morning
                     They feel just great.

BRANDER   Those two, know who they are?
                             They look foreign.
                     Think they've come far?

FROSCH   Leipzig, the city
                             They all want to see:
                     The Paris of Germany!

SIEBEL   But who do you think they are?

FROSCH   This one's down to me.
                             Tanked up
                     Nothing's an impossibility;
                     Like a rotten tooth
                             I'll dentist from their mouths
                     The truth.
                     They do look aristocratic:
                             La-di-da,
                     Definitely upper-bracket.

BRANDER   A couple of con men,
                             Running some racket.

ALTMAYER   Maybe, maybe not.

FROSCH   Watch me screw
                             These two
                     To the floor.

MEPH.   These poor
                             Insensitive fools;
                     They'd not know the Devil was near
                             If I pulled off every ear.

FAUST   Good evening, gentlemen.

SIEBEL   Evening.

                 Aside, looking askance at MEPHISTOPHELES.

That bloke's foot. It's all askew.

MEPH.   May we sit with you?
                         We've been on the road all day,
               Dreaming of sinking a glass or two.
                         And, forgive me,
               But did I hear
                         The harmony of sweet singing?

FROSCH   No doubt you're a virtuoso.

MEPH.   Talentless, but I love to give it a go.

ALTMAYER   Try us. What song you got?

MEPH.   If you wish, all the songs under the sun.

SIEBEL   Don't matter what song.
                         'Long as it's a new one.

MEPH.   We've just come back from Spain,
                         Land of wine
               Where they sing this refined refrain.

               Sings.

               There was a wise king
               Who had a big flea
                         Right up his trouser.
               He loved that big flea
                         'Dear flea let's have fun
               Come home to my housa.'

               The king told his tailor
               'Cut a gold coat
                         For my flea up my trouser,
               And a big fancy hat
                         Of an aristocrat
               For this jumping carouser.'

               Then wisely the king
               He said to his flea
                         'Be my minister regal,'
               'Thanks' said the flea

'New laws: cats, no claws
And scratching's illegal.'

The court went quite mad
With scratching the itch
      Up trousers and tights,
But said through clenched teeth
      'Oh what a relief
A PM that bites.'

But thank God that we
Are not royalty
      We're German delousers;
We squash all the fleas
      Just as we please
Right up our trousers.

FROSCH   Good song, and with a moral.

SIEBEL   Yes. If you've got to pick a quarrel,
      Pick it with something small.
Death to every flea!

ALTMAYER   Long live liberty!
      Long live wine!

MEPH.   I'd drink to that!
      If the local vintage
Wasn't such liquid garbage.

SIEBEL   Watch it, friend . . .

MEPH.   I'd treat you all to some of mine,
      But if you drink a rival wine
The landlord'll have your arse.

SIEBEL   I don't care. There's my glass.

MEPH.   Get me a wine borer.

BRANDER   What? You got
      Personal barrels o' wine
Lined up outside the door?

ALTMAYER   Behind the bar, in the box
                            On the floor . . .

MEPH.   (*Takes the tap. To* FROSCH.)
                          What wine do you favour?
                                      Of what colour, flavour,
                          Origin, bouquet of nose?

FROSCH   There's a choice?

MEPH.   Whatever goes down best
                                      At the moment of request.

ALTMAYER   (*To* FROSCH.)
                          Salivating? Can't stand waiting?

FROSCH   Rhinewine.
                                      The Fatherland's greatest.

MEPH.   (*Boring a hole in the edge of the table where*
                              FROSCH *is sitting*.)
                          Get me wax
                                      To make some stoppers, quick.

ALTMAYER   A conjuring trick . . .

MEPH.   If it works and it's wet, rejoice.
                          (*To* BRENDER).
                          Sir,
                                      The beverage of your choice?

BRANDER   Champagne. Champagne.

                          MEPHISTOPHELES *bores, in the meantime*
                          somebody has made wax stoppers and pushes
                          them in the holes.

BRANDER   Not that I don't like German wines
                                      I am a patriot;
                          A German hates the French;
                          It's just that that froggy wine,
                                      Well it's got the lot, hasn't it?
                          The champagne, very sparkling, thank you . . .

SIEBEL   (*As* MEPHISTOPHELES *is coming to his*
                  place.)
              Not dry, sweet for me.

MEPH.   The sugary wine, the great Tokay
                      Will flow for you
              In just a mo'.

ALTMAYER   No,
                          This isn't true,
              You
                          Are having us on.

MEPH.   You accuse me of some common con,
                      In front of all these gentlemen?
              Ah well,
                      The tasting will tell.

              The holes are all bored now and the stoppers
              are in their places.

MEPH.   (*With strange gestures.*)
                          Grapes swell
                          On the vine
                          Over the gates of hell;
                          The vine is wood
                          Table is wood;
                          Good table give
                          Good wine;
                          Look deep
                          Into nature,
                          See wood weep
                          Wine . . .
              Think the miracle and you'll drink it.
              Fine! Pull the stoppers and enjoy it.

              They pull the stoppers out and the wine that
              each of them asked for flows into their glasses.

ALL   Flow, fountain of wine,
                      Chilled in mountain passes,
              Into our glasses
                      And never stop.

MEPH.   Oops! Don't spill a drop.

                 They drink again and again.

ALL   Pissed like this we'd make a fist
                         Of eating up ourselves;
                 We'd be piggy cannibals,
                         With big balls,
                 Pigging up a pig.

MEPH.   When people are free,
                         Look what they want to be.

FAUST   Can we go now?

MEPH.   Allow
                         A minute more of observation.
                 You'll see the easy
                         Descent of man to bestiality,
                 Of happiness to hatred,
                         Splendidly demonstrated.

                 SIEBEL *drinks carelessly and spills some
                 wine on the floor where it bursts into flames.*

SIEBEL   Help! Fire! Help! Hell is on fire!

MEPH.   Relent, friendly element.

                 To SIEBEL.

                 Just a little free
                         Sample of purgatory.

SIEBEL   What? What you say to me? Stay
                         Where you are.
                 You're going to pay
                         For this,
                 You've picked the wrong men.

FROSCH   (*To* FAUST.)
                 No no, don't do it again.

ALTMAYER   I think . . . if we . . . just ask
                        Him to go away.

SIEBEL   Think you can come in here,
                        Trying to fool us
            With your hocus pocus?

MEPH.   You, sir, are a piss-head
                        With the body of a wine cask.

SIEBEL   What kind of crack
                        Is that?
            You deliberately insult us, you . . .
                        Quack!

BRANDER   (*Threatening* MEPHISTOPHELES.)
            You are in deep, and I mean dire,
                        Trouble, friend.

            ALTMAYER *pulls a stopper from the table,
            fire leaps out at him.*

ALTMAYER   I'm on fire! I'm on fire!

SIEBEL   Witchcraft! Black magic!
                        Quick, cut him down,
            He's a heretic.

            They draw their knives and advance on
            MEPHISTOPHELES.

MEPH.   (*With solemn gesture*.)
                        Turn illusion
                        Your other face,
                        Change mind
                        Change space.

            *They stop in astonishment and look at each
            other.*

ALTMAYER   Where are we?
                        What is
            This beautiful country?

FROSCH   Vineyards in the sun,
                        Green lines of vines . . .

SIEBEL   This land
                        Is a paradise of wines . . .

BRANDER   Squeeze these luscious grapes
                        Ripe for the picking . . .

                    He takes hold of SIEBEL's *nose. The rest do*
                    the same to each other and raise their knives.

MEPH.   Illusion,
                            Snap.
                            Surprise, surprise!
                            Enjoy
                            The Devil's
                            Joke,
                            Like a poke
                            In the eyes.

                    He vanishes with FAUST. *The friends let go*
                    of each other.

SIEBEL   You're pinching my nose.

ALTMAYER   What?

BRANDER   And you're pinching mine.

ALTMAYER   This room's going round and round
                    I've got to sit down.

FROSCH   What happened?

SIEBEL   Where is that bastard? I'll kill him.

ALMAYER   He went straight out the cellar door
                        Riding on a barrel.
                    The barrel, I saw it sort-of . . . skim
                    Along above the ground.
                    D'you think there's a drop more wine
                    In that table?

| SIEBEL | It was trickery. The swine |
| | Was a cheap illusionist. |

FORSCH   But that wine I drank was real.

BRANDER   And those grapes, you could feel
                                    'Em, so pickable
                Squeezable, eatable.

ALMAYER   Well, I'll drink to a drinkable miracle
                                    Any day!

8. Witch's Kitchen.

On a low hearth stands a large cauldron over the fire. In the steam that rises from it various figures can be seen. A female long-tailed monkey is sitting at the cauldron skimming it so that it won't boil over. The male monkey with the young ones is sitting next to her, warming himself. Walls and ceiling are decorated with strange witchcraft paraphernalia.

FAUST, MEPHISTOPHELES.

FAUST   I hate this stench
                                    Of bad black magic;
                Why drag
                Me into this madness?
                How can a witch cook
                                    Some stinking drink
                To make me look
                Thirty years younger?
                Is there nothing else on offer?
                Nothing natural?

MEPH.   If you want something
                                    Au naturel,
                It's off to the woods with you;
                                    Narrow your horizon;
                Live like an animal, rise
                                    Each morning to fertilize
                The ground on which you'd sleep,
                                    And from which you'd reap
                The vegetarian diet that you'd live upon:

The tasteless lentil
And the acorn stew.
You'd never be ill:
Then, when you were eighty,
You
Might well look thirty:
At least in the evening light.

FAUST   Can you see me on the land?
I couldn't plough a field, dig a ditch;
I work by brain, not by hand.

MEPH.   Yes, the life of a peasant:
Thoroughly unpleasant.
Ah well! We'll just make do with this witch.

FAUST   Can't *you* brew up
This cup of whatever it is?

MEPH.   Art and science are not enough,
It needs a certain fizz,
Lengthy peregrinations
Of fermentations;
A subtle this 'n' that, a whiz
Of weird ingredients.
The Devil knows the recipe,
But only a witch
Can stir and shake and make it.

To the ANIMALS.

Where is our sister?

ANIMAL   Gone up and out of the chimney,
Mister;
To a feast
With a beast:
Very, very disgusting feast
Very, very disgusting beast!

MEPH.   And how long will your mistress be,
Up and out of doors?

ANIMALS   'Til we warm our paws.

MEPH.   Dainty animals, no?
                     And brilliantly enlightening.

FAUST   They're horrible, they're stinking,
                     They're stupefyingly sickening.

MEPH.   Not at all. For me it's pure bliss
                 To have a subtly-reasoned discourse such as this.

                 To the ANIMALS.

                 Excuse me, you revolting-looking
                 Puppets of rotting meat from hell,
                     Can you tell
                 Me what you're cooking?

ANIMALS   We are cooking threadbare
                     Beggars' soup.

FAUST   Millions of customers there.

                 The MALE MONKEY *coming up to*
                 MEPHISTOPHELES, *fawning*.

MALE MONKEY
                             Dare
                                     Throw dice
                         For me?
                         There!
                                     I itch
                         For a rich
                         Win.
                                     Had I
                         Money,
                         I'd not
                                     Sin;
                         Not
                         Be mad.

MEPH.   A crazy gambler monkey? He'd really go
                     potty
                 If a monkey could buy a ticket for the lottery.

                 Meanwhile the YOUNG MONKEYS *have
                 been playing with a large globe, which they
                 now roll forward.*

THE MALE MONKEY

> Roll the world
>> Let it pass
> It's a hollow ball
> That's all;
> Easy to smash
>> As glass;
> Here a flash,
> Volcano-bright,
>> Here a light
> Of a city;
> 'I am alive'
>> It's crying;
> Keep away,
>> My son,
> It's made of clay:
> It's dying,
>> It's
> Doomed to break
> Into billions
>> Of bits.

FAUST, *in the meantime, has been standing in front of a mirror, sometimes drawing closer, sometimes stepping back from it.*

FAUST

> Who is she?
>> The woman in the magic mirror?
> How can she
>> Be as beautiful as the heavens?
> I fear her
>> Loveliness is not of this earth.

MEPH.

> Well, if a god labours away
>> For six days,
> You expect something halfway
>> Decent.
> Please, gaze
>> Upon her,
> To your heart's content.

FAUST

> My heart will tear
>> Apart;
> Madness stir

> Heat to flame within me;
Oh God, I must be there,
> Now!
I must be with her,
> Now!

The cauldron, which the FEMALE MONKEY
*has been neglecting, begins to boil over; a
great flame blazes up into the chimney. The*
WITCH *comes down through the flames
screaming hideously.*

THE WITCH   (*Seeing* FAUST *and* MEPHISTOPHELES.)
You go sneaking
> In the old crone's kitchen
You get more than you reckon;
Here's fire to burn your bones.

*She plunges the ladle into the cauldron and
splashes flames at* FAUST, MEPHISTOPHELES
and the ANIMALS. *The* ANIMALS *whine.*

MEPH.   Skeleton and abortion!
Don't you know your lord and master?
> Are you ready for a personal disaster?
Shall I shrivel you to a little snivel
> From this monkey's nose?

THE WITCH   Sorry, sorry, sorry My Lord. The human hose
> You wear
Hid your cloven hoof.

MEPH.   I'll let it go, for once.
> Today,
The Devil, too, is a victim of fashion:
It is deemed
> Culturally incorrect to display
Forked tail, horns and claws;
Even the Great Nordic Phantom
Hides away indoors.
Still, my clovenness
Can make a bad impression;
> Therefore I affect
The kind of perfect calves

Young women faint to see
When I give a dancing lesson.

THE WITCH   Oh it's really lovely to see you again,
Dear Squire Satan.

MEPH.   Woman, never use that name.

THE WITCH   Why, what's wrong with it?

MEPH.   It's a name fit
Only for fairytales;
The Evil One is banished,
But evil still prevails.
Just call me 'Baron,'
A gentleman,
Of aristocratic charms.
And here's my coat of arms.

He makes an indecent gesture.

THE WITCH   (*Shrieking with laughter.*)
Ha! Typical!
What a devil of a Devil you are.

MEPH.   (*To* FAUST.)
Voilà.   Note which way, with what or which,
One deals with a witch.

THE WITCH   Gents:
What can I get you?

MEPH.   A bottle of your famous brew,
That makes
Old humans as good as new.
But an ancient vintage;
The years double its strength
Against the ravages of dotage.

THE WITCH   Gladly. Here's a bottle
From which
I nip a little sip myself.

In a low voice.

But if this man drinks it, you know
He'll drop dead on the spot.

MEPH. He's a good friend, it'll perk him up;
Describe your circle, spin your spells,
        And give him a cup.

*The WITCH, with strange gestures, draws a
circle and puts all sorts of magic objects in it;
while she is doing this the glasses begin to
ring and the pots to hum and make music.
Finally she fetches a large book and puts the
MONKEYS in the circle, where they have to
act as a reading-desk for her and hold the
torch. She beckons FAUST to come to her.*

FAUST (*To* MEPHISTOPHELES.)
What is this
        Mockery?
It's crazy.
I hate this crass
        Trickery.

MEPH. Do you or do you not
        Want her to make the elixir?
Then tolerate her appalling sense of theatre;
As a herbalistical, shamanistical,
        Black-magical specialist,
Hocus pocus
        Helps her focus.

*He makes FAUST step into the circle. The
WITCH recites from the book with great
emphasis.*

THE WITCH   Make one out one then
        End up with ten;
        Add nought to three
        And be wealthy,
        Lose the four
        And end up poor;
        Take five from six and seven
        And eight won't go to heaven;
        So when nine takes one

Ten ends up none.
There. Magical mathematical tables, done.

FAUST   The old woman's completely out of her head.

MEPH.   On the contrary. I've read
          This book,
And it's all like that; page after page.
I've lost an age,
          Oh, several thousand years,
Studying it.
          The mystery of contradiction
Can be an addiction
          To the genius and the fool.
The Art, my friend, is both old and new;
By it you concoct
          Endlessly clever-clever
Theories and phrases,
          Pseudo philosophies
To pull the wool
Over the eyes of the reader;
Everyone has the utterly
          Unjustified feeling,
That words must have meaning.

THE WITCH   (*Continuing.*)
          The world can't find
                The secret of the art;
          But the man who can't think,
          And the man who's got no heart,
          Will find it in a wink.

FAUST   What's that gibberish meant
          To mean?
Oh! A hundred thousand fools in a circus tent
          Swish
About in my head.

MEPH.   Enough, wise oracle,
          Motherly nipple
Which succubi suck upon;
Pour this man a tipple
          Of your potent potion.

*THE WITCH, with great ceremony, pours the
potion into a cup. As FAUST raises it to his
lips a pale flame arises.*

MEPH.   For a couple more of the same,
                        You think you can make
                 A friend of the Devil,
                        And not get burnt by the flame?

*The WITCH opens the circle. FAUST steps
out of it.*

MEPH.   On we go! Don't stop!

THE WITCH   (*To* MEPHISTOPHELES.)
                 Hope my little drop
                        Has the right
                 Effect.

MEPH.   Many thanks, old thing;
                 I owe you a favour:
                        Why not collect
                 On Walpurgis Night?

FAUST   The woman I saw,
                        Too beautiful to be real:
                 Let me see her in the mirror
                        Just once more . . .

MEPH.   No, soon you'll see
                        The real thing;
                 The perfection of womanhood
                        In the flesh.

Aside.

                 Drugged up with that, my boy,
                 Every woman will be
                        A Helen of Troy.

9. Street

FAUST. MARGARETA *passing by.*

FAUST	Lovely lady, don't run away; Let me walk a little, Talk a little with you.

MARGARETA	I'm not lovely, I'm not a lady, Go away.

She frees herself and walks away.

FAUST
> Beauty, purity
>   Yet
> A hint of something
>   Saucy,
> Her red lips,
> Her downward look
> As she moved,
>   The air
> Flowing over her hips;
> My heart is a book,
>   She rips
> It page by page.
> That girl?
> Get her for me.

MEPH.   Girl?

FAUST   That girl.

MEPH.
>   Oh *that* girl:
> She's just been to church.
> I sneaked by
>   That spiritual urinal
> Catholics call the confessional
> And overheard her with her priest.
> So innocent
> She had nothing to confess.
>   She even leaves me
> Powerless.

FAUST   But she's over fourteen?

MEPH.   Ooh, the talk
                    Of a Don Juan who believes
             There is nothing so sweet
                    It can't be licked;
             No flower so pretty
                    It can't be picked.

FAUST   Are you suddenly
             A master of Arts in Morality?
                    Listen to me:
             I have her tonight
                    Or we
             Finish at midnight.

MEPH.   Be reasonable,
                    I'll need two weeks;
             The seduction of the seemingly unseducable
             Is technically highly tactical.

FAUST   I don't need the Devil's powers
             To seduce a slip of a thing
                    Like her;
             Just give me seven hours.

MEPH.   Spoken like a Frenchman.
             But, with respect,
                    What good is
             Wham-bam thank-you-very-much sex?
             Consider the more exquisite aspects;
                    Making
             A deliciously elaborate plan
             Like the plot of an Italian novel,
                    Pulling the little doll
             This way and that, kneading
             Her like dough, before the moment
                    Of hot baking.

FAUST   I don't need all that.
             I'm hungry enough for her already.

MEPH.   Seriously, with this child
                    Take time. No wild
             Gesture; be cunning,
             Move like slowly moving slime
             Toward her.

FAUST   Get me something to give her. Now.

MEPH.   A present! Good. Success
                     Will come with tactical thinking.
                             I'll do some checking;
                             Look up my index
                     Of buried treasure.
                     Wait! What's this I find?
                     Why, a box
                             I stuffed with goodies earlier;
                     A present
                             To take the breath away,
                     To dazzle the mind;
                     I got it for another woman,
                             More worldly, much maturer,
                     I didn't know you'd go
                     For the innocently pubescent.

FAUST   You think I should give it to her?
                             You think I . . .

MEPH.   You want to keep the treasure
                             For yourself?
                     I do it all
                             For you, get the girl jewels
                     Whisper thoughts of you to her,
                             Nudge her toward her fall;
                     And what do you do?
                             Look the grim professor
                     Walking into a lecture hall.
                     Let's go!

10. Evening

A small, tidy and clean room. MARGARETA *is braiding and binding her hair.*

MARGARETA   I wish I knew
                     Who that man was today;
                             So good-looking,
                     And the bold way
                     He spoke to me
                             Must mean

He's a gentleman of quality.
It's so close in here, so sultry.

She opens the window.

And yet it's
          Not that warm outside.
I feel so . . .
          I don't know.
Mother, come home.

She begins to sing as she undresses.

> The King of Thule
> A worthy ruler
> Had a lover
> Who, sadly, died;
>
> And as she died
> The King of Thule's
> One true lover
> Gave him a cup:
>
> A golden drinking cup.
> And when he came to sup
> The king would drink
> Just from that drinking cup;
>
> And when that ruler
> Came to die,
> He gave up
> All but her cup:
>
> For one last time,
> With all his friends,
> He drank a drink
> To all that ends;
>
> Then threw the cup
> Into the sea:
> The cup was full
> And so was he.

*She opens the cupboard to put her clothes in
and sees the jewellery box.*

Who's that?
            Who hid
That here? I've never seen
Such a lovely box;
            It must have been
Left with my mother
As a pledge for security
            Oh! The lock's
Open
It's full
            Of jewels!
Jewels for a rich,
            For the highest
Noble woman;
How would that necklace
            Look on me?
If I could keep
            Just those earrings.
Who owns
            These wonderful things . . .
What did they put
            Them here for?
What's the worth
Of only being young and pretty?
People praise you
            Out of pity.
God have mercy
            On we, the poor.

11. A Walk

FAUST *walking up and down in deep thought.* MEPHISTO-
PHELES *joins him.*

MEPH.   By bitter, bitched-up lost love,
                    Stars above
               And all the fires in hell:
               What worse curse
                    Can I use?

FAUST   Bad news?
                    What an evil look
               Even for the Devil!

MEPH.   Yes, I could easily let myself go to the devil,
        If I wasn't.
    The jewels I planted
        For Margareta;
    They've ended up in other
        Hands. Wait for it:
    The fat hands of a priest.
    It's the girl's mother. She sees
    The jewellery, sniff's evil's handiwork
        And goes berserk.
    That woman's nose
    Is always stuck in a prayer book,
        She can smell
    A piece of furniture
    And tell if it's
        Sacred or profane;
    She gives the jewels a sniff
    And gets a full whiff
        Straight from hell.
    'My child', the pain
        In the arse intones,
    'Ill-gotten wealth
        Destroys the health
    Of the soul;
    We'll give this to the blessed Mary
    And she will pray for us.'
    Little Gretchen bites her lip
        And wants to make a fuss;
    'It's a gift,' she thinks,
        She can't see how
    The giver of the gift
    Can be *so* very godless.
    But the Mum calls the priest,
        Whose eyes have a feast
    Calculating cash value;
    'Let us pray,
    The giver is blest!'
    Cries this unctuous
        Man of God;
    'Holy church has a stomach
        That can digest
    Continents and nations,
        Huge donations
    Of cash, yet never has belly pains;
    The church alone has the constitution

To stash away ill-gotten gains.'
And he hooks the bracelet,
The necklace, the ring,
The diamond locket
Into his pocket
                As if they were nothing;
Dishes out a blessing
And leaves the ladies
                Feeling uplifted.

FAUST   And Margareta?

MEPH.   Is restless, frustrated,
                Confused; she can
            Think of nothing but the jewels
                And the mystery man
            Who sent them.

FAUST   My poor abused, distressed
                Darling . . .
            Get her more jewels!
            Anyway, that first lot were poor;
                Get better jewels,
            Get double what she had before,
            Get them now.

MEPH.   Anyhow,
                Just out of the air?

FAUST   Do it. And get in the favour
            Of the woman next door.
                Move, devil!
            Keep to the rules
                Of our contract,
            Serve me,
                Get more jewels for her!

MEPH.   Certainly, glad to be of service,
                My dear sir.

            Exit FAUST.

            A love-sick fool
                Will go to any extremes,

He'd blow up the sun,
> The moon and stars,
Just for a smile
> From the woman of his dreams.

11. The Neighbour's House

MARTHA God forgive my husband;
Out of the blue,
Not a sorry or a thank you,
> He just upped
And left me lying in the straw;
What did I do wrong?
> I obeyed his every whim.
I'm still in love with him
I cry my eyes raw.

She cries. She snaps out of it.

Maybe he's dead. Oh God.
If only I had a death certificate.

MARGARETA *enters.*

MARGARETA Martha!

MARTHA Gretchen, what is it?

MARGARETA My legs are giving out
> Under me;
Amazingly,
> There was another box
In my cupboard;
> Ebony, and very heavy,
Full of lots more
> Than the other one.

MARTHA This time, don't
> Tell your mother; she'll go
Holy on you again and throw
This one to the priests as well.

MARGARETA Look, look.

MARTHA   Oh you
Lucky girl.

MARGARETA   I wish I could show them off;
          Dance in them, whirl
Along the street, go
To church in them, kneel
          In prayer,
With beautiful diamonds
Shining in my hair.

MARTHA   No, be discreet,
          Come and see me:
Wear them in front
          Of my mirror,
We'll enjoy them secretly.
There'll be the odd occasion,
A saint's day, a celebration
          When you can wear
A pearl in your ear,
          A sparkling ring here, the glory
Of a necklace there.
Your mother won't notice,
Or we'll make up some story.

There is a knock.

MARGARETA   Oh God, is that my mother?

MARTHA   (*Peeping through the curtains.*)
It's a man. I don't know him.
          Please, come in.

MEPHISTOPHELES *enters.*

MEPH.   I ask forgiveness for my boldness,
          Ladies.

On seeing MARGARETA *he steps back
respectfully.*

I came to see
          Mrs. Martha Schwardtlein.

MARTHA   I am she, what you do want?

MEPH.   Pardon me, you are busy
                    With a lady of nobility;
            I'll call later.

MARTHA   Listen to that!
                    The gentleman thinks
            You're an aristocrat.

MARGARETA   I'm a poor girl, sir;
                    You're very kind,
            But the jewels aren't mine.

MEPH.   It's not the jewels that shine,
                    It's what they decorate:
            You are as bright
                    As the light of a sunny day.
            Thank you *so* much
                    For letting me stay.

MARTHA   Do you have something to tell me, or . . .

MEPH.   Madam, if only I came to your door
                    With happier tidings:
            Your husband is dead
                    And sends you his greetings.

MARTHA   Dead? My husband dead?

MARGARETA   Dear Martha, oh dear lady . . .

MEPH.   Let me tell you the sad story.

MARGARETA   I never want to be
                    In love; to lose
            The one I love
                    Would kill me.

MEPH.   Each need will feed
                    Upon another:
            Joy needs sorrow,
                    Sorrow joy.

MARTHA   Tell me where, why, how.
                        Tell me now.

MEPH.   I stood at the head
                        Of his deathbed;
              It was cheap, indeed
                        Something of a dung heap,
              Made of stinking, rotten straw;
              Though he died a sinner
                        And a Christian,
              Cursing his life
                        As a bit of a dog's dinner.
              He cried:
                        'Why did I leave my wife?
              The memory is killing me!
                        Can she forgive me
              But . . . '

MARTHA   (*Weeping*.)
              The good man, he didn't know
                        I forgave him
              A long time ago . . .

MEPH.   . . . 'But, as God is my witness,
                        It was her fault
              I walked out.'

MARTHA   What a lie.

MEPH.   No doubt out
              Of his head with delirium.
              His death-bed, last gasp and testament
                        Continued:
              'I was ready to slave
                        For her;
              For the house and the children;
                        I gave and gave.'

MARTHA   So he forgot all my married fidelity,
                        All my drudgery.

MEPH.   On the contrary, he thought of you dearly.
              He said:
              'When I left the island of Malta

I said a little prayer
For my family,
      And God rewarded me:
We captured a Turkish ship
      Stuffed with the Sultan's treasure;
Rare jewels, gold, and ivory;
      I got my share
And skipped my ship in Italy.'

MARTHA   His share of treasure?
      Could it be
Buried in Italy?

MEPH.   Buried, spent, stolen,
      How can we know?
I am sorry to cause you sorrow.
Your husband came to Naples,
      Where he met an Italian beauty,
And, losing all sense of duty,
      Entered bigamous nuptials.

MARTHA   What? How dare
      That bastard!
Marry another
And with treasure to spare;
Robbing his children, robbing me,
      Leading a life of sin?

MEPH.   Why else is he in a coffin
      Rotting as we speak?
I suggest a period of formal mourning,
      Then seek
A new lover.

MARTHA   I'll never find another
      Sweet and beautiful
As him: pity he was a gambler
      And a liar,
A constant traveller,
      A bigamist
And always pissed.

MEPH.   Marriage to you
      Sounds a rather good deal.

Would the same conditions apply
    If *I*
Were to kneel
    And pop the question?

MARTHA   Oh, sir. Are you teasing me?
    I don't think I heard . . .

MEPH.   (*Aside*.)
Whoops! Mistake.
    This one could make
Even the Devil keep his word.

To MARGARETA.

And you, my dear,
    Are you in love?

MARGARETA   What do you mean?

MEPH.   (*Aside*.)
Ah, pure white dove.

Aloud.

Goodbye, ladies.

MARTHA   One more thing, sir;
I like things sewn up neat.
    I can't sit
Easy, you know, not knowing
How and when he died and where;
I mean, what I really want
    Is to read it
In the local paper;
Then I'll know he's dead, properly.

MEPH.   Luckily
I have a friend. He was there too
When death's curtain
Was drawn across your unfortunate late
                    husband's
    Unfortunate life.
We'll go up before a judge:

Two witnesses
Of the truth?
The Death certificate is certain.
I'll bring my friend round
To you.

MARTHA   Please do.

MEPH.   And will this lady condescend
To meet my friend?
He's a fine man, very polite.

MARGARETA   I don't think it's right.
Meeting a stranger, that kind of
thing . . .
Makes me blush.

MEPH.   You could stand, unflushed, unblushed
Before a king.

MARTHA   Bring the gentleman,
But we'll have to be discreet.
We'll wait
In my garden, near the gate.

12. Street

FAUST, MEPHISTOPHELES.

FAUST   When's it going to happen? Now? Soon?

MEPH.   Tonight. Violins, full moon
Etcetera.
At Martha's, her neighbour.

FAUST   Right. Right.

MEPH.   But first, Martha wants a favour.

FAUST   Why not? She's doing us a good turn.

MEPH.   We must provide
                      A water-tight, above-board
             Death certificate,
             Testifying
                      Her husband's bones
             Rot happily in Padua,
                      In consecrated soil.

FAUST   Very clever.
                      First a long journey
             To Italy;
             For how long? Two
                      Months?

MEPH.   Santa simplisimus.
                      No need to go abroad.
             We'll do
                      A straight-forward fraud.

FAUST   That's just squalid.
                      Call the whole thing off.

MEPH.   Oh, holy man:
             What, have you never lied, not just a little bit?
                      Never born false witness,
             Never a hint of the hypocrite?
             I've heard you sound
                      Off about God,
             Nature and man,
             Occupying
                      'The moral high ground',
             I've heard you applaud
                      Religion;
             But, deep down,
                      Did you believe it?
             Weren't your teachings
                      A fraud?
             Come off it,
                      You lied;
             What's the difference
                      Lying about
             How some worthless nonentity died?

FAUST   But you will always be a liar
                      That's your nature.

MEPH.   Tomorrow you will swear
That, why!
            You love her
With all your heart,
And you and she will never part.
There!
        Do I lie?

FAUST   No.

MEPH.   But to seduce
            The little thing,
When you swear
            Eternal love and honour
Won't you be lying?

FAUST   I am in love with her.
What I feel
            Is real
But it's true
I depend totally
            On you
To win her for me.

13. A Garden

MARGARETA *walking up and down with* FAUST, MARTHA
with MEPHISTOPHELES.

MARGARETA   You're just saying that,
You're just
            Being kind,
Flattering me;
A man with a mind
            Like yours,
Can't find
Anything I say entertaining.

FAUST   One word from you
            Entertains more
Than all the wise words
In all the libraries of the world.

He kisses her hand.

MARGARETA   Don't kiss it.
                        My skin's rough.
            My mother's
            Strict:
                        She keeps me in,
            Working hard.

            They pass on.

MARTHA   And you, Sir, are you
                        Always travelling?

MEPH.   True,
            I am professionally peripatetic,
                        Never static;
            Yet what a pain it is to leave
                        Certain places;
            As soon as you unpack a case
                        You repack it.

MARTHA   It's alright when you're young
                        And free,
            Going off to the far-flung
            Corners of the earth;
                        But the bad times come:
            Still single and you're forty, fifty,
                        Dragging yourself to the grave,
            Old and so lonely.

MEPH.   An experience
                        Coming to me.

MARTHA   Take my advice then, Sir, marry.

            They pass on.

MARGARETA   Yes, at home
                        Out of sight, out of mind;
            But, sir, you're polite
            Because you know the right
            Thing to do,
                        In the company
            Of clever people.

FAUST   My sweet one, what people call 'clever'
                        Is usually feeble
               Vanity, showing-off.

MARGARETA   Really?

FAUST   Why do simplicity and innocence
                        Never know
               The sacred power of their influence?
               Humility, modesty,
                        These are gifts
               Of nature, that we . . .

MARGARETA   Do you ever
                        Think about me?
               I think about you, every
                        Moment of the day.

FAUST   My dear, yes, of course I think of you.
                        Are you . . .
                                Alone a lot, then?

MARGARETA   Our household is small,
                        But there are all
               The chores to do;
                        We don't have a maid
               So all day I go
               Round and round;
                        I cook, clean, sew.
               My mother's very
                        Pernickety;
               We don't have to live
                        Economically,
               We're better off
                        Than some
               My father left us a little
                        House outside the city
               With a garden;
               But, yes, I've learnt to settle
                        For a pretty
               Quiet life;
               My brother is a soldier;
                        My little sister
               Is dead. She was a handful,

But she gave me
Joy in my heart;
I'd give anything,
Do all that hard work
All over again,
To see her living.

FAUST   She's an angel singing
In Heaven,
If she was like you.

MARGARETA   Mother was too
Ill to bring her up,
So I did. She loved me,
Oh so much.
Mother couldn't feed her,
Couldn't do
A thing for her;
So I would give her
Milk and water;
Then she became
My own darling,
In my arms, on my lap,
Wriggling and smiling
As she grew.

FAUST   You must have felt the purest
Happiness.

MARGARETA   Yes, but what was hardest
Was . . .

They pass on.

MARTHA   But women are at a disadvantage;
Bachelorhood is baggage
A man doesn't want to lose.

MEPH.   He can learn;
He needs a good teacher
To relieve him of his burden.

MARTHA   But seriously, sir,
Have you found no one?
You've never lost your heart?

MEPH.   One has been told
                            A good wife, house, and regular
                                                dinners
                   Are worth all the gold
                            In the world.

MARTHA   But you have never been inclined?

MEPH.   I've always got on famously,
                            When I've wined and dined
                   The occasional lady.

MARTHA   I mean, inclined to pop the question.

MEPH.   I find it advisable
                            To never *seriously* trifle.

MARTHA   You don't understand me.

MEPH.   I'm terribly sorry,
                            But I do.
                   I understand that you
                            Are trying to be helpful.

                   They pass.

FAUST   So, my little dove,
                            The second
                   I came into the garden,
                   You recognized me?

MARGARETA   I thought
                            Oh will he
                   Find fault,
                            Think I'm rude?
                   First time I saw you
                            In the street
                   I dreaded that our eyes would meet;
                   But they did . . .
                   And half of me
                            Said 'Am I
                   Leading him on?'
                   Then that thought was gone;
                   And I was angry

> With myself
> For not being angry at you.

FAUST   My dear sweet love,
        What can I say? . . .

MARGARETA   Wait!

She picks a marguerite and pulls off the petals one by one.

FAUST   What's this, a bouquet?

MARGARETA   Just a game.
Don't laugh at me.

She murmurs as she picks off the petals.

FAUST   What?

MARGARETA   (*Half aloud.*)
Loves me, loves me not . . .

FAUST   An angel's face, what purity . . .

MARGARETA   Loves me . . . not . . . Loves me . . . not . . .

She pulls off the last petal, exclaiming with child-like joy.

He loves me?

FAUST   Yes, my child,
        He loves you.
Do you know
What that means?

He takes both her hands.

MARGARETA   I'm trembling.

FAUST   No trembling,
        Feel the warmth

In my hands; they are saying
More than words can say:
>Give yourself completely,
Live in an ecstasy
>>That lasts forever.

MARGARETA *presses his hands, frees herself and runs away. For a moment he stands lost in thought, then he follows her.*

MARTHA   Night is falling.

MEPH.   Yes and sadly
>We must go.

MARTHA   I'd say stay longer,
But this garden's a gossip trap;
>Neighbours at every window
Watching you,
Itching to tell lies.
>Where have our couple
Got to?

MEPH.   Fluttered up that garden path,
>Like butterflies.

MARTHA   He likes her, I see.

MEPH.   And she him;
>The old, old story.

14. A Summerhouse

MARGARETA *comes running in, hides behind the door, puts a fingertip to her lips and peeps through a crack.*

MARGARETA   He's coming.

FAUST   (*Entering.*)
Little rogue,
>Now I've got you,
No escaping now.

He kisses her.

MARGARETA   (*Embracing him and returning his kiss.*)
Dearest man, how
            I love you.

MEPHISTOPHELES *knocks.*

FAUST   (*Stamping his foot.*)
What's that?

MEPH.   A friend.

FAUST   A beast.

MEPH.   Time to be running along.

MARTHA   (*Entering.*)
Yes sir, it's late.

FAUST   Can I walk you home?
            At least
To the garden gate?

MARGARETA   My mother, I told you she'd kill me.
            Goodbye.

FAUST   Must I go?
            Well, goodbye.

MARTHA   Adieu Monsieur.

MARGARETA   I'll see you again, soon, goodbye.

FAUST *and* MEPHISTOPHELES *leave.*

Dear God what wonderful, wild
            Things a man like that can say;
And I go to pieces, I
            Say 'yes' to everything.
I'm ignorant, I'm just a child;
            What can he see in me?

15. Forest and Cave

FAUST   (*Alone.*)
                 Sublime spirit, all I ever prayed for
                 You have granted me. You looked at me
                 From within the fire and gave to me
                 All of nature's splendour for my kingdom;
                 The senses to enjoy and relish her;
                 And you do more than merely show me
                                                  pictures,
                 You bless me with the power to see deep
                 Into her heart; you show me how I'm one
                 With all creatures, in woods and sea and air;
                 And when the storm roars within the forest
                 And the giant spruce falls and crushes
                 Nearby trees and branches, and the hills
                 Boom with thunderous echoes from the crash,
                 You lead me to the safety of a cave,
                 You show me to myself, you reveal
                 Mysteries and wonders to my heart.
                 And when, as I gaze transfixed, the moon
                 Slides up into the night, pale silver shapes
                 Float down the rocks and up from forest
                                                  thickets:
                 The silver spirits of lost and ancient worlds
                 Come to soothe my troubled contemplation.
                 Now I understand perfection's not
                 For man; together with this ecstasy
                 Which lifts me ever nearer to the gods,
                 You gave me this companion, with whom
                 I cannot do without, even though
                 He degrades me in my eyes, coldly
                 Turning all your gifts into nothing
                 With a simple cynical word. And he
                 Has lit a fire inside me for her beauty;
                 I reel; I lust, and gratify myself;
                 And, gratified, I burn with lust again.

MEPH.   (*Enters.*)
                 What a terrible life style;
                          Doesn't it sap
                 All the fun away?
                          A bit of a wallow
                 In lust and love's fine for a while;

But it's time to snap
Out of it.

FAUST   I wish you had
Something better to do.
I was enjoying a moment's peace
Without you.

MEPH.   A touch tetchy, are we?
I'd gladly
Leave you alone;
I'm run ragged all day long,
Fingers worn to the bone,
The cringing servant in his place
Trying to read his master's face;
You feeble,
Ungrateful, miserable, weedy
Human specimen,
But for me
You'd be in
Your grave by now, you fool.
You've still got him in you,
The scholar, the intellectual.

FAUST   If the devil
Had the shred of a soul,
He'd understand the inspiration
Of a walk on a mountainside,
How I draw new strength, new happiness
From walking in this wilderness.

MEPH.   Ah, heavenly,
Inspirationally supernatural
Insightful-type happiness,
Ecstatic excesses
Embracing the earth;
One feels oneself
Swelling up divinely;
Sucking the earth's marrow
Tortured by thirst
For knowledge,
Feeling the six days of creation
Beating in your heart,
Pumped up near to burst,

No more a part
Of humanity,
Overflowing with ecstasy,
To bring, at last, the lofty fantasy
            To climax with . . .

With a gesture.

Shall we say
            What's to hand?

FAUST   Don't be disgusting.

MEPH.   Oh oh! Do you
                        Swing enough moral clout
            To shout
                        'Disgusting'?
            Chaste ears
                        Are not allowed to hear
            What the hypocrite heart
                        Can't do without.
            Back to the nitty gritty.
                        Your sweetie,
            Your pretty bit,
                        Sits alone in her room
            Locked in adolescent gloom.
            It's you
            That's on her mind.
                        You really should
            Learn to ration
                        Your blind passion;
            Down it rushed upon her
            Like a little stream,
            Bursting its banks in spring
                        With snow water,
            Pouring all over
                        The dear sweet thing;
            And now your stream
                        Is a little dribble again.
            I think instead
                        Of all this head activity,
            Your majesty
            Should leave lofty thoughts
                        Of the mountains above

And look to the poor little monkey,
        Hugging her misery,
And give her some love.

She stands at the window
        So low
In herself,
        Watching clouds
Drift over
The old city wall,
She sings, so prettily,
        So soppily,
'If I were a dove',
        All day and half the night.
She does cheer up, now and then,
But not very often;
        Her eyes soften
With weeping,
Her nails dig into her arm;
She howls again and again
        Then is suddenly calm.
She is so much in love.

FAUST   Snake. Snake.

MEPH.   (*Aside*.)
             Yes and I've snared you.

FAUST   Get away from me
                  Monster;
             Don't mention
                  That beautiful woman;
             Don't make me a madman
                  Again,
             Mad for that body.

MEPH.   What, then?
             She thinks you've run away;
                  And she's halfway
             Right.

FAUST   We're together even though apart,
                  Close though far away;
             Wherever I am my love slips

Into her heart;
I'm even jealous
    Of the image of Christ
When she touches his lips.

MEPH.   Ah, I envy you.
'Two young roes that are twins, which feed
                    among the lilies.'
Forgive me, is it libel
    For me to quote the Bible?

FAUST   Get away. Pimp.

MEPH.   Ah, insults.
It's an enjoyable diversion
    Making lovers
Lose all sense of proportion.
The God who made little girls and boys
    Honours the noble profession
Of match-making; He enjoys
To see us pimp
    A great beauty
To some limp
    Inadequate.

FAUST   The joys of heaven,
All the charms
    Of religion, fail
When I sleep, held in her pale
    Arms.
But even when I lie on her breast
Don't you think I feel her distress?
Am I not a fugitive,
    Homeless,
A monster not fit to live,
    Doomed to reel
Around the world without rest,
    Roaring like a waterfall
From rock to rock,
Desperate for the shock
    Of the fall
Into the great abyss?
For it was I,
    The godforsaken,

Who brought her to this,
    My vice
That destroyed her peace.
Hell you had to have this sacrifice!
Help devil, devil, cut
    This fear short!
Abort
    Time;
What has to happen
    Make it happen now;
Let us rush
    To our end,
Come, Fate, crush
    Her, crush me, now.

MEPH.   Boiling again?
    Is it all aglow
Down below?
Oh . . . just go
    And be nice to her;
Only a pea-brain, lovesick idiot
    Can't see an exit
From the obvious problem,
    And becomes apocalyptic.
Buck up, don't care;
    Only the brave get lucky!
There's a devil in you too;
And there's nothing more tasteless
    Than a devil in despair.

16. Gretchen's Room

GRETCHEN (MARGARETA) *is alone at her spinning wheel.*

My peace long gone,
My heart will burn
    He'll not return,
Never forever.

All madness;
Into the grave;
    Nothing can save
A world in pieces.

My peace long gone,
My heart will burn;
       He'll not return
Never forever.

I look out of windows,
Walk in the street,
       Only to meet
And see him again.

His bright eyes;
His funny walk,
       His magic talk
Delighted me;

The press of hands,
The touch of lips,
       Pleasure that slips
From tongue to tongue . . .

My peace has gone;
My heart will burn;
       He'll not return
Never forever.

If I could see him,
I'd hold my breath
       Would gladly die,
Kissed to death.

17. Martha's Garden

MARGARETA, FAUST.

MARGARETA   Promise me, Heinrich!

FAUST   I promise. Ask away.

MARGARETA   Then: tell me,
       You're a good man, and clever,
    But is it true
       You
    Don't believe in God?

FAUST   All that matters is I love you,
                 And for those I love I'd die.
                 I don't want to
                          Rob the faithful of their faith;
                 And I don't want religious strife
                          Ruining my love-life . . .

MARGARETA   You must believe it's true!

FAUST   Must I?

MARGARETA   I don't think you respect
                          The holy sacraments, either.

FAUST   I do.

MARGARETA   But you've no desire
                          To go to mass;
                 And when did you last confess?
                 You're not . . . a denier . . .
                          My dear, you do believe in God.

FAUST   Darling, who can say
                          'I believe in God'?
                 Ask the priests, ask the scholars;
                          The answers
                 Mock you for asking.

MARGARETA   I'm asking
                          You, though.
                 Do you believe?

FAUST   Please, don't misconceive
                          What I say,
                 My dear;
                          But who can say
                 God's name
                          And claim
                 'I know God!'?
                 And who can
                          Deny
                 His name, and say 'I
                 Know there is no God!'?
                 The one who enfolds

The universe,
                Doesn't he hold
You, me and himself
In the great scheme?
                Isn't the high caverned
Roof of Heaven
                Above us;
Isn't the earth
                Fixed beneath our feet?
Don't the eternal stars
Rise to meet
Our eyes at evening
                With a smile?
And while
                We look
Into each other's eyes,
                Isn't everything
Crowding,
                Spinning
In your head
                And round your heart,
Weaving its mystery
                In you and me?
Fill your being,
                Drink
In this happiness,
Then, call it what you like:
                Ecstasy, joy,
Heart, happiness, love, God!
I have no name for it;
Feeling is all,
                All is feeling;
A name is merely sound and smoke,
Obscuring true meaning.

MARGARETA   That's what the priests
                    Sort-of say,
             And when I listen
                    To you it sounds fine;
             But it can't be true
                    Because you're not a Christian!

FAUST   Oh little one . . .

MARGARETA   And I hate that man
         Who's always with you.

FAUST   Sweet thing,
         Don't be afraid of him.

MARGARETA   When I see him I freeze;
         When he's near
I feel a strange terror;
There's always a sneer
         On his face,
Mockery in his eyes,
         He will despise
Anything good;
It's written on his forehead:
         He loves no one,
He wants we who do love, dead.
In your arms I'm warm and happy,
         I feel free;
When he's here
         I panic,
I feel choked with fear.

FAUST   Oh my visionary angel.

MARGARETA   It's hateful;
         He's here every day;
He only has to come through the door
         And I feel
I don't love you any more;
And another terrible thing:
         When he's here
I can't pray.
It scares
         Me so; Heinrich,
Can you say your prayers?

FAUST   You just don't like him very much.

MARGARETA   I've got to go.

FAUST   Will I ever spend
         One whole
Hour in your home,

> Lying upon your bosom,
> Breast to breast,
> Soul to soul?

MARGARETA   If only I slept alone;
> But you know mother
Sleeps in the same room.
I'd leave the door
> Open tonight,
But my mother's a light
> Sleeper:
And if she caught us together
She'd kill me, there and then.

FAUST   Darling, I
> Can arrange that;
See, this little bottle; three drops
> In her drink
And she will sink
Into a deep and peaceful sleep.

MARGARETA   I'd do anything for you;
But will it hurt my mother?

FAUST   Oh my sweet, would I ever
> Hurt someone you love?

MARGARETA   Dear man,
> One look at you,
One touch
> Of your hand
And I find I do
> Anything you want;
I've done so much,
What can I do more?

She exits. MEPHISTOPHELES *enters.*

MEPH.   Little monkey-face,
> What,
Slipped out the door?

FAUST   Spying again?

MEPH.   Saw and heard the lot.
                         She blows
               Hot and cold;
                         A slip of a girl's got
               You, the bold
                         Super-sensual, would-be worldly
               Seducing suitor,
               Led about by the nose!

FAUST   Freak, monster, accident
                              Of nature, born out
               Of fire and excrement.

MEPH.   And monkey face
               Is good at physiognomy;
               One glance at me
                         Makes her feel all wobbly;
               Her sixth sense
                         Gives her a sniff
               Of a great presence
                         Behind this human mask;
               Dare she ask if
                         I am a genius,
               Or even the Devil . . . ?
               Ah well . . .
                         Is tonight the big night?

FAUST   What's that to you?

MEPH.   I want a good time too!

18. At the Well

MARGARETA *and* LIESCHEN *with water jugs*.

LIESCHEN   Did you hear about
                         Barbara?

MARGARETA   No. I hardly go out
                         At all.

LIESCHEN   Eating for two.

MARGARETA   Oh dear.

LIESCHEN   It's true!
                           Doesn't it stink?
                   She had it coming,
                           Throwing
                   Herself at that man.
                   Barbara, always
                           had to be first;
                   Conceited about her beauty,
                           But fawning
                   On presents from him.
                   What cuddling and kissing;
                           Well, he well and truly
                   Tricked her,
                           And now her
                   Flower is picked forever.
                   What do you think?

MARGARETA   I think . . . poor girl.

LIESCHEN   You're not *sorry* for her?
                   When we were
                   Slaving at night at the spinning wheel,
                   Barbara was up a dark alley,
                           Slobbering
                   Over her fancy man,
                   Lifting her skirt.
                   Well, now she can
                           Pay the penalty:
                   It'll be
                           Church and bended knee,
                   Penance in a hair-shirt.

MARGARETA   But he'll marry her.

LIESCHEN   Don't be a fool.
                   A man like that's got one rule:
                   Don't stay,
                           Get in and out then run away.

                   MARGARETA, *walking home.*

MARGARETA   I used to burn
                           With indignation

When some poor girl went astray;
I was so self-righteous,
                    Saying 'Whip the hussy
In the street.'
And now it's my turn;
                    Now gossips will say
Horrible things about me.
                    But oh, oh, the sin:
It was . . . so . . . sweet.

19. A Cathedral

Service with organ and choir. MARGARETA *in a large congregation.* MEPHISTOPHELES *is behind her.*

MEPH.   And how does it feel,
               Gretchen, going up to kneel
               Before the altar,
               Now that you've done the act?
                    Not the same?
               Horribly not at all the same
               As before,
               When you were oh so fully holy,
               Innocent,
                    Intact?
               Sh, rude of me;
                    You're saying
               A little prayer. I wonder,
                    Can it be
               For the soul of your mother?
               Whom you sent
                    Down to torment?
               Have you dug her dried blood from under
                    Your fingernails yet?
               And in your heart
               What is it you sense?
                    What stirs,
               What squirms,
                    What swells
               In you,
                    What terrifying
               Presence?

MARGARETA   Mother of sorrows,
                          Have pity, have mercy;
              Look down at my agony
              Oh Mother, what
                          Can atone
              For my sin?
                          Every bone
              In my body
                          Sings with pain.

CHOIR   Dies irae, dies illa
              Solvet saeclum in favilla.

              Organ.

MEPH.   Wrath tears
                          At you;
              The trumpet
                          Blares;
              The dead
                          Turn
              In their graves;
              Your heart
                          Rises
              From its ashes,
              To burn
                          And burn
              Again,
                          Eternally,
              In pain
                          And dread.

MARGARETA   The organ music
                          Sucks my breath away;
              The singing
                          Eats my heart like acid;
              I'm sick,
                          I can't stay . . .

CHOIR   Judex ergo cum sedebit,
              Quidquid latet adperebit,
              Nil inultum remanebit.

MARGARETA   I can't breathe;

The roof vaults
>Press down,
The walls squeeze
>In . . .
Please! Please!
>Air!

MEPH.   Squeezing
>But no hiding
Of your sin and shame;
>Endless blame
But no air,
>Endless night
But no light,
Not for the likes of you.

CHOIR   Quid sum miser tunc dicturus?
Quem patronum rogaturus,
Cum vix justus sit securus?

MEPH.   The redeemed
>Cannot bear to see
Your face,
The pure
>Can't bear to be
Near you:
>No redemption, no purity
Not for the likes of you.

CHOIR   Quid sum miser tunc dicturus?

MARGARETA   (*To a* NEIGHBOUR.)
Please, the vaults are . . .
Do you have smelling salts, I . . .

She faints.

20. Night

In the street outside MARGARETA's *door.* VALENTIN *a
soldier and* MARGARETA's *brother.*

VALENTIN   When the lads are being bores,

All well away, drinking and toasting
        The women in their lives, getting hot
Under the collar, boasting
'My girl's better than yours,'
        No she's not, yes she is, no she's not'
I sit, elbows
        On the table, calm and dignified;
Then I raise my glass and say
        'No way
One girl's beauty cannot be denied:
Gretchen, my little sister.'
And it's click, click, clinking and drinking
        'Here's to Gretchen
The loveliest, the purest
        And the best.'
And now?
I'm a bad joke,
        The bloke
Whose sister . . . it drives me crazy,
Any bastard can come up to me
        And have a poke;
And I'm 'sposed to sit there
        Like a lemonhead,
Grinning at anything that's said.
I'd like to smash
        Their faces to bits.
And why don't I? Why?
'Cos the glove fits.
        'Cos I can't say they lie.
Who's that?
        Two of 'em.
If it's him,
        I'll tear his head off.

FAUST *and* MEPHISTOPHELES *enter.*

FAUST   See how the lamp in the sanctuary
        Flickers in the church window,
Darkness presses
        Upon its fragile flame.
I feel the same
        Pressure of dreadful night
Upon my heart.

MEPH.　　　　And I
　　　　　　　　　Feel like I'm a thin little cat,
　　　　　　Padding over roofs:
　　　　　　A desire
　　　　　　　　　For the virtues
　　　　　　Of lechery and thievery
　　　　　　　　　Burns inside me;
　　　　　　My limbs are on fire
　　　　　　　　　my claws
　　　　　　　　　Twitch with delight;
　　　　　　It's forty-eight hours
　　　　　　To wonderful, wonderful
　　　　　　　　　Walpurgis Night.

FAUST　　　　No jewellery,
　　　　　　　　　No ring?
　　　　　　It upsets me
　　　　　　To go to her with nothing.

MEPH.　　　　Gifts were how
　　　　　　　　　We got her started;
　　　　　　She'll do it for nothing now.
　　　　　　I know what:
　　　　　　　　　I'll sing
　　　　　　A little moral song
　　　　　　To chivvy her along.

He sings, accompanying himself on the guitar.

　　　　　　What are you doing,
　　　　　　Lovely little Kate,
　　　　　　　　　By your lover's door,
　　　　　　Early in the morning?

　　　　　　Sweet Kate don't do it
　　　　　　Don't knock upon that door,
　　　　　　　　　You'll go in a maid
　　　　　　And out a maid no more.

　　　　　　Careful, my dear Kate
　　　　　　Once it's eaten up
　　　　　　　　　You can't rebake
　　　　　　Your tasty little cake.

And girls, a thief
Before he steals a thing
     Must slip a ring
Upon a pretty finger.

VALENTIN *steps forward.*

VALENTIN   Who you trying
            To catch?
Child snatcher,
          I know what you are:
The Devil can have your guitar
          And the singer.

VALENTIN *smashes* MEPHISTOPHELES's
guitar.

MEPH.   You rearranged my Stradivarius.

VALENTIN   Now I'll rearrange you.

MEPH.   (*To* FAUST.)
Doctor, to us,
          Hurry,
Out
          With your feather duster;
A quick and violent flurry,
You strike I'll parry.

VALENTIN   Parry this!

MEPH.   Give us a kiss.

VALENTIN   This one.

MEPH.   Having fun?

VALENTIN   Who am I fighting, the Devil?
          My hand's gone numb . . .
I can't stand,
          Nothing's level . . .

MEPH.   Stick it in him, pull it out.

VALENTIN   Oh God . . .

MEPH.   One more lout
                        Down the hole.
                And now we run:
                I'm very friendly with the local police;
                        Sadly, the magistrate's
                Not on the payroll.

MARTHA   (*At her window.*)
                Wake up! Wake up!

GRETCHEN   (*At her window.*)
                Get a light.

MARTHA   There's a fight
                In the street!

THE CROWD   There, there's one
                        Lying on the ground . . .

MARTHA   Murderers! Did they
                        Get away?

GRETCHEN   (*Coming out of the house.*)
                Who's lying there?

THE CROWD   Your mother's son.

GRETCHEN   Valentin. Valentin.

VALENTIN   It's a simple thing,
                        It's nothing,
                Dying? Quickly
                        Done.
                No fuss, no crying,
                        No women wailing.
                Gretchen,
                        Listen.

                They gather round him.

                Everyone can tell

> You're new at the game;
> But since you want to be a whore
> > It's a shame
> Not to do it well.

GRETCHEN
> Brother, what are you saying,
> > Oh my God . . .

VALENTIN
> God? God's got nothing to do
> > With this bad joke
> You've played on me.
> But what's done is done,
> > You will be what you will be:
> First one man,
> > Then two,
> Then a dozen,
> > Then every bloke
> In this city
> > Will have had you.
> And every decent citizen
> Will shrink
> > From you;
> You will be the stink
> From the gut
> > Of an infected corpse;
> When they look into your eyes
> You'll see how they despise
> > You, you slut;
> For you
> No walk up the aisle,
> > No ring,
> No white veil,
> No dancing at your wedding;
> In some vile
> > Corner of the city
> You'll wail,
> Hidden amongst the worst
> > Dregs of humanity;
> Even if God's pity
> > Reaches you,
> On earth you'll be cursed.

MARTHA
> Don't talk so
> > About what God will do,

That's blasphemy;
Make your peace and ask for mercy.

VALENTIN   You vile, pimping old prostitute,
                    If I could get at you
                I'd ring your neck;
                    Then do
                All the penance in purgatory I had to.

GRETCHEN   Brother,
                    Don't torture
                Yourself and torture me . . .

VALENTIN   Save your breath;
                You broke my heart,
                    End of story.
                I die a soldier and a good-enough man,
                    So now I can
                Sleep in death,
                Hoping to wake in God's glory.

                He dies.

21. Walpurgis Night

The Hartz Mountains, near Schierke and Elend. FAUST,
MEPHISTOPHELES.

MEPH.   We've still got oodles
                    Of country to cover;
                How about
                    A ride on my poodle's
                Back? Or a broomstick?
                I know, a leaping,
                    Randy little billy goat
                Will do the trick.

FAUST   As long as my legs are up to it,
                    And I've got a strong stick,
                I'm happy
                    To walk;
                First, the labyrinth of the valley;
                    Then the long

Climb to this rock, over it a stream
     Cascading down;
The birches are stirring with spring,
The spruces feel the sap rising;
     Just the thing
To put some zip into a day's walking.

MEPH.   Give me winter, I'm lost
Without a touch of frost;
I like a stab of ice in my insides,
The crisp
     Crunch of snow . . .
Whoops! Can this be right?
Suddenly it's night;
How mournfully the half-moon
     Rises, its dull red light
Dim and feeble . . . Darkness hides
     The way; you could bump
About all over these rocks, and fall;
I know! I'll call
     A will-o'-the-wisp.

FAUST, MEPHISTOPHELES, *and the*
WILL-O'-THE-WISP *sing in turns.*

MEPH.   It seems
We have entered
A world of magic,
And dreams
Lead us along
The air that races
Through these wild
Open spaces.

ALL   Uh-hooo, what a row
All the birds make;
Screech owl, lapwing, jay
Are you still awake?
And are there salamanders
Sliding in the grass?
Roots, like writhing snakes,
Shoot up tentacles
Round the feet and ankles
Of the wanderer,

Tight as manacles;
And amongst the heather
Hordes of multi-coloured mice
Scatter hither and thither;
And the glow-worms fly
In clouds of great profusion
Increasing our confusion;
Are we standing, sitting,
Walking, running, spinning?
Rocks and trees pull faces
The swarm of glow-worms races.

MEPH.   Isn't Mammon making the palace
Blaze spectacularly!
You'll be lucky to see
Flashy hellish lighting at its best.
Already I feel the rest
Of the wild company.

FAUST   Violence, the storm's bride,
Rages through the air, where
Can we hide?

MEPH.   Save yourself,
Cling on to this shelf
Of old rock, or
The ravine will be your grave.
A mist thickens the night;
Owls fly about in fright;
The pillars of tall
Ancient palaces of green
Are splitting and creaking;
The screen
Of branches is torn;
Mighty tree trunks fall
Booming through the wood; roots yawn,
Wrenched from the soil
And, terribly tangled, all
Crashes down together.
This is
Wonderful weather!
The wind howls and hisses
Raging and wrecking
The ravines; can you hear the voices

In the sky?
Near, now far away? All along
          The mountain
A magic chant
          Pours out, a fountain
Of furious song.

WITCHES   (*In chorus.*)
                    Crops green, stubble yellow;
                    Hello
                              Says the witch
                    With a rich
                              Fart;
                    Then she winks
                              'Cos the billy goat
                    Stinks.

                    The road wide, the road long;
                    A prong
                              Of a pitch fork:
                    Baby goes
                              Squawk;
                    Baby cursed
                              And baby's mother
                    Burst.
                    The stars in, the wind still,
                    An ill
                              Moon is hiding;
                    What's flying
                              Fast?
                    Bright sparks fly,
                              Witches are roaring
                    Past.

HALF-WITCH   (*From below.*)
                    Stop! Stop!

SECOND VOICE (*From above.*)
                    Who calls from the crevasse?

HALF-WITCH   Don't leave me behind!
                    I've been climbing up
                    Three hundred years;
                    I want to sup
                    With you witches, my own kind.

BOTH CHORUSES
                    Broomstick,
                              Stick,
                    Pitchfork,
                              Billy goat:
                    All carry, fly and float.
                    Climb up,
                              Slime up,
                    Hump up,
                              If you can't
                    You're for the high jump.

HALF-WITCH   I waddle, I toddle, I fear
                              I just can't catch up;
                    I'm fed up
                              At home,
                    But I don't belong here.

                    They sit down.

MEPH.   What joshing, pushing,
                              Rushing, rattling!
                    Hissing, darting,
                              Pulling, prattling!
                    Glowing, sparking,
                              Stinking, burning!
                    This is the world of witches,
                              Their true element.
                    Hang on to me
                              Or we'll lose each other.
                    Oh, where
                              Are you?

FAUST   (*From a distance.*)
                              Over here!

MEPH.   What, over there?
                              Grab me, doctor, hold on,
                    One leap and we'll be gone
                    Out of this whirling morass
                              Of wildness in the wilderness,
                    It's too much, even for me;
                    Down there, I see a strange glow
                    In the bushes, flickering invitingly;
                              Come on! That's where I want to be.

FAUST

Spirit of contradiction, lead on then;
            Though I'd rather be
Up there on the mountain
            Look! Fire and smoke twist
In whirlwinds;
            Look! That devil and that witch
Kissed:
            Now hand in hand they run
To greet the evil one;
            If only I was running with them,
Think of the knowledge
            That could be won;
Ignorance would be dissolved,
            And all the riddles solved.

MEPH.

Only to get fooled and tangled up
            In new ones,
Diddled and re-riddled.
Let's have a little sit-down. Here's a cosy spot.
Oh what do I see? Why what a lot
            Of young witches,
All rudely naked and nakedly rude,
            All utterly desirable.
Relax, don't be unsociable.
            Damn, I hear music;
I always hate music;
Screaming and croaking
            Like a half-eaten frog,
Being sicked-up by a cat . . .
Still! Got to put up with that.
            Move! Move!
No choice, no choice, got to;
In we'll go
            I'll introduce you;
And bind you to me
            All over again,
Fresh and new;
Peep inside and see
            A hundred fires burning;
Here it's all dancing wild reels,
Cooking elaborate meals,
            You can dance, eat,
Make love;
            What could be a better treat?

MEPHISTOPHELES *speaks to a group sitting around dying embers.*

MEPH.

Gentlemen, why sit
       Out of the dancing,
So full of groans and moans?
I'd love to see you in the thick of it;
       Raucous, roaring youth prancing
Around your old bones.

A GENERAL

You can't trust the government;
Forget the medals you won,
       The songs sung
In praise of your achievement;
A nation's like a woman,
       She only loves the young.

A POLITICIAN

We've lost our way; I praise
       The good old days:
It was a golden age then,
When we were powerful men.

A PARVENU

We were sharp, we'd chop
       All that was old to get to the top;
But now the world's gone strange,
We just want change to stop.

AN AUTHOR

Literature? What's the use?
In the future, who will need
       A well-written book?
The young just want to look
       At scenes of violence and abuse.

MEPHISTOPHELES *suddenly seems very old.*

MEPH.

People, I see, are ripe for judgement day
       As I climb
Up witch-mountain, one last time;
I am an old camel
       The fat in my hump
Dried-up; and the moment I die, why
       It's the last trump.

A PEDLAR-WITCH

> Gents, I'll tell you what I'll do;
> > For you,
> Buy one and have one more
> > Absolutely free;
> Everything's a fine and genuine antique
> But, I admit, sadly
> > Not unique;
> There's not a thing here
> > You've not got on earth;
> Not a knife
> > That's not stabbed a wife;
> Not a cup that's not
> Poured hot
> > Poison into a husband;
> No jewel that's not led
> > A lovely lady
> To a seducer's bed;
> No sword that's not
> > Been unkind,
> Breaking a truce
> > Or killing a friend
> From behind.

MEPH.

> Dear cousin, my dear
> > Would-be sales-pitch witch,
> I fear
> > Your goods are past it;
> Forget antiques, it's novelties
> We want,
> > Novelties we itch
> For: only the new will do!

FAUST

> Who's that woman?

MEPH.

> Yes, look at her
> > With care.
> That's Lilith.

FAUST

> Lilith . . .

MEPH.

> Adam's first wife. Beware
> > Her silken hair
> That dresses

> Her beautiful body;
> If she tangles those long tresses
> Round a man,
> > He'll never get free.

FAUST *dances with a* YOUNG WITCH.

FAUST

I had a little dreamy
> Of an apply tree;
Two little wellple apples,
> Just for me;
Uppy wuppy I climbied
> Up that apply tree.

THE YOUNG WITCH

Naughty-waughty men
> Think applies very nice
Ever since
> Life in naughty paradise;
Want to see the apply
> Growing in *my* garden?

MEPH.

I dreamt a mad tree,
> Split into two;
There was a big hole in that tree,
> And the bigger that hole
The better for me.

THE OLD WITCH

Greetings old hellish mole
> Knight of the cloven foot;
You'll need a great big plug
> To put in that great big hole.

MEPH.

(*To* FAUST, *who has stopped dancing.*)
Why let that lovely girl
> Go?
She looked so charming,
> Singing while you were dancing.
You were getting on like a house
> On fire.

FAUST

Yes, I was full of desire
> And just about to kiss her,
When a little red mouse
Popped out of her mouth.

MEPH.   What's a touch of bad breath
                      Between lovers?

FAUST   But then I saw . . .

MEPH.   Yes?

FAUST   She's still there.
              Mephisto, that beautiful girl,
                      Pale as death,
              Who hovers
                      At the edge of the dancing,
              So lonely,
              Dragging her feet slowly,
                      As if they were misshapen,
              Or . . . no, chained . . .
              Is she chained?
                      Oh, have I regained
              My sweet love?
                      Is she Gretchen?

MEPH.   Look away, you fool,
              It's a dangerous illusion,
                      A magic apparition,
              A lifeless, gorgeous
                      Nothing.

FAUST   It's true, her eyes are dead,
              Dead as the eyes of a corpse;
                      But that's the breast
              She offered me
              As we lay upon her bed.

MEPH.   That's witchcraft,
                      Don't be so gullible;
              The magic art
              Makes her appear
                      To everyone as their sweetheart.

FAUST   But what pleasure
                      I gain
              In the pain,
              I can't look away;
              Her lovely neck displayed

> With a red ribbon
> > No wider than a knife's blade.

MEPH.   You like that? Do
> > You want to see her
> With her head off too?

22. A Gloomy Day. Open Country

FAUST, MEPHISTOPHELES.

FAUST   How can I live with myself? The beautiful,
                 sweet, poor creature, locked away like a
                 common criminal? Is this what it's all been
                 for, you treacherous, despicable demon? She's
                 arrested, in prison, in desperate misery. And
                 what do you do? Keep it from me, sweet-talk
                 me, lull me with idiotic, tasteless sideshows.
                 What were you going to do? Let her die,
                 wretched and alone?

MEPH.   She's not the first one to go that way.

FAUST   You dog. Revolting . . . Oh Great Spirit, turn
                 this monster, this huge, disgusting worm, back
                 into that dog, that poodle, when he thought it
                 was funny to roll about at the feet of some
                 unsuspecting traveller. Change him back to his
                 favourite shape, so I can kick him, 'til he rolls
                 whining on his back in the sand. 'Not the first
                 one . . . '. I find the misery she must be feeling,
                 the suffering, beyond human comprehension.
                 The marrow of my bones melts at the thought
                 of the misery of one, just one, in her predica-
                 ment, but you, you calmly sneer at thousands.

MEPH.   Millions. Oh dear, here we are again at the end
                 of our tether, at the point where you humans
                 always go to pieces. Why do you get involved
                 with us, if you can't see it through? You want
                 to fly but you've got no head for heights? Did
                 we force ourselves on you, or you on us?

FAUST   Don't gnash your teeth at me, it's nauseating.
         Great and lofty Spirit, why have you chained
         me to this vile companion, who delights in
         destruction and gloats over ruin?

MEPH.   Have you finished yet?

FAUST   Save her.

MEPH.   'Save her.' Wait a moment, who was it who
         ruined her in the first place? Me or you?

         FAUST *looks around him wildly.*

MEPH.   What you doing, looking round for a
         thunderbolt? Wise move not to give that
         particular device to wretched mortals, like
         you. A philosophical discussion would
         become a nightmare; smashing an opponent's
         head off with fire and brimstone, on account of
         a tiny little critical remark? Very tyrannical.

FAUST   Take me to her. She is going to be free.

MEPH.   And your personal danger? Remember, you
         did do her brother in. They're out for your
         blood in that city. You wouldn't believe the
         look of the avenging spirits, hovering over his
         grave, waiting for you to turn up.

FAUST   May all the murder, all the death of the world
         fall on you, you monster. Take me there. Free
         her. Now.

23. Night. Open Country

FAUST *and* MEPHISTOPHELES *storming past on black horses.*

FAUST   What's that, circling around
                     Hanged man's hill?

MEPH.   No idea, but I guess
                     They're stewing and cooking up a mess

Of something to make someone
Deliciously ill.

FAUST   The sky's filled
               With them floating up, floating down.
                    Bending and bowing.

MEPH.   It's a Witches' Guild.

FAUST   What are they worshipping,
                    What are they blessing?

MEPH.   On on, ride on.

24. Prison

FAUST *with a bundle of keys and a lamp, in front of a small
iron door.* MARGARETA *sings from inside.*

MARGARETA   My mother was a whore
                             She killed me;
                        My father was a thief
                             He ate me;
                        My little sister kept my bones
                             Secretly
                        And I became a forest bird;
                             Now I fly
                        High and faraway and free.

               FAUST *unlocks the doors and enters.*

MARGARETA   (*Hiding herself on the mattress.*)
               They coming, they're coming, they're going
                    To kill me.

FAUST   (*Softly.*)
               It's alright, it's alright. I can set you free.

MARGARETA   (*Rolling herself in front of him.*)
               Aren't
                    You human?
               Can't
                    You see my agony?

FAUST   Quiet! You'll wake the guards.

He takes up her chains to unlock them.

MARGARETA   Did you win at cards
                        To be the one to come for me?
               Hangman?
                        Why at midnight?
               Isn't the morning
                        Soon enough for you?
               I'm so young to die,
                        And I was beautiful, too;
               My lover was near
               Now he's far away;
                        The bouquets of flowers
               Are withered and dried . . .
               He was going
               To make me his wife . . .
                        Let me go!
               Don't be
                        Violent with me.
                        I've never seen you
               In my life.

FAUST   The strife in my heart,
                        The pain
               Rips into me.

MARGARETA   I'm totally
                        In your power,
               Mister Executioner.
               I'll be meek, I'll be mild;
               But just let me
                        See my child;
               You know they hid
                        It?
               Then they came and said
               'You killed the kid',
                        Just to be cruel.
               They sing that old song
               About me,
                        'The Fool
               And The Devil's Baby';
                        But that can't be
               The right story,
                        Not about me.

FAUST   (*Throwing himself at her feet.*)
                 Gretchen, I'm kneeling
                          Before you;
                 I've come to free you
                          From this terrible place.

MARGARETA   Yes, we all must all kneel to face
                          The saints,
                 'Cos human blood paints
                 Those steps over there;
                          Look under,
                 But beware:
                 Hell's boiling
                          In the cellar,
                 The devil's roaring
                          And coiling
                 His tail
                          In anger.

FAUST   Gretchen! Gretchen! Stop it!

MARGARETA   (*Suddenly attentive.*)
                 That was my lover's voice.

                 She jumps to her feet. The chains fall off.

                 To be free.
                          I would rejoice,
                 And fly to his arms.
                 He called out 'Gretchen'.
                          He stood
                 On the threshold of my hell,
                          Through the yell
                 And rattle,
                 The terrible row
                          Of the hatred of demons,
                 Somehow
                          He called to me.

FAUST   Gretchen, you *are* free.

GRETCHEN   It is you.

FAUST   Come on, come with me.

GRETCHEN   No, stand still,
                         Let me fill
               My mouth with kisses.

FAUST   We must hurry,
                         Or we'll be lost.

GRETCHEN   No kiss?
               You don't make sense.
               Why am I so tense
                         In your arms?
               What is it I miss?
               Before, I felt
                         A whole heaven
               Open and overwhelm me,
                         All restraint
               Broke:
                         You kissed
               As if
               You wanted to choke
                         Me.
               My love? Kiss me
                         Or I'll kiss you.

               She embraces him.

               Your lips are cold.
               Why do you look so ashen,
                         Who has taken
               Your love from me?

FAUST   I'll love you with all the passion
               Of all of high heaven,
                         But please, now,
               Don't you see? All I want
                         Is you to follow me.

MARGARETA   Is it you?

FAUST   Yes! Yes!

MARGARETA   You press
                         Me to you again;
               But then,

> You don't know whom you're setting free,
> My friend.

FAUST   Come, or the night will end . . .

MARGARETA   I killed my mother and I drowned my child.
>   Wasn't that little biddy baby
> Given to you, as well as to me?
> Touch me. No. Please understand,
> I'm very shy.
>   But why
> Is there blood on your hand?
> I beg, I beg you, say
>   You'll put your sword away.

FAUST   Let the past die.
>   You are killing me.

MARGARETA   No, you have to be alive;
> The graves must survive,
>   Well-tended for.
> My mother
>   In the best one,
> Then, not far away,
>   My brother;
> Me, a little further on;
> And the little one
>   Right by my side.
> No one else;
> I used to snuggle
>   Up to you,
> That was sweet happiness;
> But now I have to press
>   Myself to touch you;
> Like there's a force
> Pushing me away;
>   Yet you say
> You're you,
> And you look like you.

FAUST   Please, walk out of here with me.

MARGARETA   Out there?

FAUST   Into freedom.

MARGARETA   If there's a grave
                                      Waiting for me
                     Then I'll come,
                                      But I'll keep
                     To one path: from here
                                      To eternal sleep.
                     What, are you going? Oh Heinrich, Heinrich,
                     If only I could just walk out of that door.

FAUST   You can. Want it that bit more
                                      And it will happen.
                     The wretched door is open.

MARGARETA   I mustn't. What hope is there?
                                      Running away,
                     Dragging through each day;
                     What'll I be?
                                      A beggar
                     In a foreign country,
                     Clothes and conscience
                                      Threadbare.
                     And they'll catch me anyway.

FAUST   I'll be with you.

MARGARETA   Go! Quick!
                     Save your poor child!
                     Up
                                      The stream
                     Over
                                      The footbridge
                     Into
                                      The wood;
                     Left by the fence;
                     In the pond
                     Good
                                      And fond
                     Father, see
                     Your little baby wriggling
                                      Sinking
                     Down
                     Don't let him drown
                     Save him . . .

FAUST   Stop it, come to your senses,
                 One step and you're free.

MARGARETA   Up here on the mountain
                         I feel so alone.
                 I feel as cold
                         As the dead.
                 Look, there's my mother sitting on a stone,
                         Wagging
                 Her head.
                 She doesn't wave, or nod, or scold.
                 Her head's too heavy
                         She's so sleepy
                 She'll not wake up again.
                 Remember that time when
                         She didn't wake up
                 And we made love and were *so* happy?

FAUST   If I can't beg you, I'll carry
                 You away.

MARGARETA   Don't touch!
                 I hate violence.
                         Insolence!
                 And I did so much
                         For you.

FAUST   The dawn is coming.
                 My darling . . .

MARGARETA   Daybreak and last day.
                         This was going to be my wedding day.
                 Don't tell a soul
                         You and I made the two-backed beast.
                 I'll see you again
                         But not at the Wedding feast.
                 The crowd is gathering,
                         So many people,
                 The town is bursting;
                 Not a word is spoken;
                         The bell is tolling,
                 The rod is broken;

They're seizing me,
   Binding me;
Now they're forcing me
   Down upon
The block;
And the sharp blade is rising
Above all the faces in their places,
And the world
   Is silent as oblivion.

FAUST   I wish I had never been born.

MEPHISTOPHELES *appears outside the door.*

MEPH.   Doctor! You've got to get
      Her out by dawn.

MARGARETA What's he
      Doing in this holy place?
Don't let him see my face;
      He's after me.

FAUST   You're going to live.

MARGARETA Lord God, I give
      My spirit to your judgement.

MEPH.   (*To* FAUST.)
Come! Or I'll abandon you
      And you can share her torment.

MARGARETA Save me, my Lord;
      Sublime horde
Of angels, standing at the gate
Of heaven, enfold me, keep me far
      From the Evil One;
Heinrich, you make me
      Shudder with fear.

MEPH.   She's been judged, sentenced, and condemned.

VOICE   (*From above.*)
She is redeemed.

MEPH.   (*To* FAUST.)
               Come come come come come to me.

               He disappears with FAUST.

VOICE   (*From within.*)
               Heinrich, Heinrich . . .

FAUST

PART TWO

ACT ONE

I. 1 A Pleasing Landscape

FAUST, *lying in a flowery meadow, weary, restless, longing for sleep. Dusk. A circle of spirits, in swaying motion, graceful little figures.*

ARIEL   (*Sings, accompanied by Aeolian harps.*)
     Spring rains of blossoms are falling
     In the green and gleaming
       Bright morning,
     And mortals wake with hope
       Of a new beginning,
     And elves that are tiny
       But fierce in spirit,
     Rush to help the evil sinner
       As much as the saint,
     Loving the loser as much as the
       winner.

     You who circle the air
       Around his head,
     Repair
     The damage wrought by the terror
       At what he has done and seen;
     Calm his dread, clean
       His soul; remove the red hot arrows
     Of reproach from his harrowed heart.

CHORUS   (*Solo, two, or more, antiphonally and all
     together.*)
     Cradle him,
       Let him sway
     In a child's sleep;
     Close the gates of day
       To his weary eyes;
     Night falls, soon

The dim splendour
            Of the moon will rise;
The hours will fade away,
            Pain and joy will cease.
Feel it, feel it,
Peace will return to you;
You will be well again;
Trust the new day,
Throw the empty shell
            Of troubled sleep away:
Only the daring man succeeds,
So wake and greet the blazing sun,
There are great deeds
            Waiting to be done.

A great roar heralds the approach of the sun.

ARIEL   Listen to the storm of the hours
                            Drumming, pounding
                The ears of earth's spirits;
                The new day is being born.
                A loud music rises,
                            Light itself is sounding
                Bright as an orchestra of brass.
                The wheels of the sun's chariot pass
                Crackling along mountain ridges, then roar
                            Up into the sky,
                To dazzle the eye,
                            Astound the ear.

FAUST   The beat
                            Of the pulse of life
                It's there, it's there, it greets
                The sweet
                            Ethereal dawn.
                Earth,
                            You were faithful
                Through the night;
                Refreshed, you are breathing
                            At my feet
                And beginning
                To enfold me with joy,
                Stirring in me,
                Inspiring in me,

A hard determination:
To strive
To the highest
Existence;
To be
Truly alive.

Look up! The gigantic mountain peaks
Foretell the great moment
Of the dawn's birth;
The eternal light
Hits them first;
Then down it comes,
Down to the valleys,
Banishing shadows
Down, down, step by step;
The sun is out walking
In the green meadows!
The shining clarity
Of the new day
Blinds me;
I have to turn away.

And that is what it's like;
The great wings
Of the gates of fulfilment
Swing
Open and hope,
After its long struggle,
Stands at last before
The ultimate success;
But an excess
Of flames flares
From the eternal depths,
Fear sears us;
We want to light
The torch of life,
But a great
Wave of fire
Engulfs us.
Is it love or is it hate
Which blazingly
Entwines us?
Joy and pain alternate
Terrifyingly;

We can only
                Look to the earth again
To hide beneath
                Its green canopy.

So, I'll keep my back to the sun
And celebrate
                The glory it illuminates;
The waterfall,
                The downward crash
Of cataracts
Falling in thousands of streams,
                To smash
On the rocks below,
The frothing spray glittering;
Then, in this chaos
                Of water and light
The rainbow arches its glow
                Of colours;
Sometimes it's clearly drawn,
Sometimes it wavers
                Then disappears
Into the air,
                Cool showers flying from it.
The rainbow is a mirror
                Of human ambition;
The life for which we are striving
                Is a fleeting
Coloured reflection.

I. 2   Imperial Palace

*The Throne-Room. Council of State awaiting the Emperor.
Trumpets,* COURTIERS *of all kinds splendidly dressed. The*
EMPEROR *makes his way to the throne, with the* ASTROLOGER
on his right.

EMPEROR   Greetings, loyal and dear friends.
                I see a wise man at my side,
            But where's my jester?
                Has he decided to hide?

SQUIRE   He collapsed behind you
                 In the procession;
                          Just out there, on the stair.
                 The huge fat gut was carried away:
                 Drunk or dead,
                          It's hard to say.

SECOND SQUIRE
                 Then, out of the blue,
                          Another jester pushed through
                 And took his place.
                 And what a jester!
                          It's hard to imagine
                 Anything more grotesque.
                 There he is! The guards
                          Have got the joker!

MEPH.   (*Kneeling at the throne.*)
                 What is desired,
                          Yet is always rejected?
                 What is feared,
                          Yet is always protected?
                 Whose reputation
                          Is the lowest of the low,
                 But whom everyone
                          Wants to know?
                 And though it warns
                          All to leave it alone,
                 What is it you call, oh Emperor,
                          To the steps of your throne?

EMPEROR   Too many riddles.
                          These clever
                 Gentlemen have brought enough riddles
                          To last forever.
                 My old jester's gone off somewhere;
                 Come, sit by me;
                          Ease the imperial
                 Wear and tear.

                 MEPHISTOPHELES *climbs up and crouches
                 at the left side of the* EMPEROR.

THE CROWD   (*Murmuring*.)
             A new fool . . . how miserable . . .
             Doesn't it make you sick . . .
             The old one was fat
                       As a barrel . . .
             This one's
                       Thin as a stick.

EMPEROR   So tell me why,
                       When we should be
             Under a sunny sky,
             Enjoying the season of carnival,
             We are tormenting ourselves
                       With the funereal
             Business of having to sit
                       In a state council.
             But, since you all insist,
                       I suppose we must get on with it.

CHANCELLOR   A halo
                       Shines above the imperial head,
             The glow
                       Of the greatest virtue;
             Only he
                       Can give it to his people:
             Justice.
                       But what is
             The use of reason to mind,
             Goodness to heart, willingness
                       To hand
             When a sickness
             Rages through the land;
             Crime? Evil breeds
                       Evil;
             One steals cattle, another a wife;
             Another cross, candlestick and chalice
                       From a church;
             The criminal boasts
             No one can touch him;
                       His victim
             Queues in the hall
                       Without redress
             Ignored
                       By judges on their satin cushions;

And the state
    Is doomed to lurch
From one mess
To another, from riots to rebellions
In a torrent
    Of abuse and hate.
The rich who offend
    Boast that money can bend
A court their way;
    Only the innocent,
Who can't pay
    A famous lawyer his fat fee,
Are ever found 'Guilty'.
Good men, with the best intentions,
    End up grateful for the pensions
Doled out by the bad.
And, in the end,
The judge who cannot punish
    Will finish
In league with those
    He could have condemned.
Do I paint a bleak
    Picture?
It could be bleaker still.

A pause.

Sooner rather than later, we will
    Have to act;
When all
    Are both criminal and victim
The state will crack
And the throne itself will fall.

COMMANDER-IN-CHIEF
    Wild days filled
        With anarchy;
All orders are disobeyed,
It's kill and be killed;
Citizens barricade
    Their houses,
Knights fortify
    Their rocky castles;
All defy us;

The mercenaries
>Won't fight if we don't pay,
And if we pay
>They'll run away;
They've wrecked
The Empire we paid them to protect;
All is pillaged, derelict;
Other countries, other kings
>Have seen
Our plight, but turn away
Too terrified to intervene.

TREASURER   Never believe the lies
>Of allies;
The tap is turned,
>No water flows;
Promised loans
>Fail to materialise.
Your majesty,
>Where has all the money,
All the property
>Of the country gone?
Certain 'parties'
Know where it goes;
It's an old, old story,
Everyone scraping and hoarding;
Wealth flows
To the private chamber of gold
At the expense
>Of public glory.

SENESCHAL   We want to economise
>But always overspend,
And, in the end,
>What have we got?
Not enough wine.
There used to be
>Hoards,
Cask upon cask of fine
>Vintages,
But thanks to the ravages
>Of the endless drinking
Of the Lords
>It's all been drunk;

And now we're all ill
Drinking beer
      From the cellar
Of the city council.

EMPEROR	Fool? What about you?
	     Do you have a favourite whinge
	To add to this binge
	     Of misery?

MEPH.	I've no complaint at all.
	     I am happy
	To observe the pall
	     Of splendour
	About your majesty;
	The rule of natural power
	     Falls like a shower
	Of gentle rain,
	     Dissolving all hostility,
	Watering imperial diversity;
	Where reason and goodwill
	     Reign, what treacheries
	Could combine
	     To bring darkness,
	Where the imperial stars shine
	     So brightly?

CROWD	A flatterer . . .
	     A wheedler . . .
	A joker . . .
	Is there a plot? . . .
	     Who's he got
	Behind him?

MEPH.	Where in this world
	     Is there no want?
	No one wants for nothing,
	     Everyone wants something;
	Here the want is . . . more, lots more,
	     Money.
	Not to be
	     Just picked up off the floor,
	It's true;
	But wisdom is about revealing

What is deeply hidden:
Underground
          In mountain veins, deep rocks,
Gold can be found.
If you ask me who can find
          It, I say;
Trust the gifted man's
Power over nature
          And force of mind.

CHANCELLOR Nature and mind?
                    Unchristian ideas.
            Root them out!
            Nature is sin,
                    Mind the Devil;
            They breed
                    Their hideous, wild
            Hermaphrodite child,
                    DOUBT.
            There are two pillars
                    Of society,
            Army and clergy;
            They alone
                    Protect the vast panoply
            Of the imperial throne;
            They run the church and state
                    As their just reward.
            But doubt and intellect
                    Confuse the mob,
            And opposition ferments;
            The sorcerer and the heretic
                    Wreck
            Town and countryside,
            And you, joker, snide
                    Poker
            Of fun, spreader
                    Of slander
            Against all that is noble,
            You keep evil company,
            The depraved, the degenerate
                    Are a fool's family.

MEPH.   I see you are
                    A man of learning;

What you can't touch
        Must be miles away;
What you don't know
        Must be nonsense;
What you can't weigh
        Must be weightless;
What you can't buy
        Must be worthless.

EMPEROR   Why this Lenten sermon?
This endless analysis
        Is a bore.
We need money,
        Therefore:
Get it.

MEPH.   I will get more,
        Much more, even, than the more
You want, your majesty.
It's easy; but, like all that's easy,
        It's nigh-on an impossibility.
It's lying there
        In front of you,
But getting it's the hard part,
        That needs art.
Think how,
        In the bad years,
The terrible times
        Of senseless crimes,
When refugees
Swamped the country,
How this one, and that one,
Overcome with fears
        For their property,
Hid their treasure away;
It's been done
        For centuries,
From the Romans to today.
There it lies, unspent,
        Buried in the ground.
The Emperor's ground.
        He shall have it!

CROWD   For a fool,

He's bright . . .
That is the Emperor's right . . .

MEPH.   And if you don't trust
                    This poor joker,
             Here's just
                    The man for you,
             An astrologer!
                    He knows the whir
             Of orbits, the mechanism
                    Of the houses of the hours;
             Tell us, magister, of the powers
                    Of heaven.

The ASTROLOGER *speaks,*
MEPHISTOPHELES *prompts.*

ASTROLOGER   The sun is of pure gold;
             Mercury the messenger
             Will fly above the sky;
             Venus lovely lady
             Looks at you charmingly,
             Morning and evening;
             Luna is moody;
             Mars threatens with might
             Jupiter gives beautiful light;
             Saturn is big
             But small to the eye,
             As a metal he is puny,
             In Value small, in weight heavy;
             But when Sol joins with Luna
             Gold with silver
             All things can be possessed:
             Palace and glorious garden,
             Rosy cheek and pretty breast:
             All this be done
             By a powerful one
             Come to cure our ills.

CROWD   What's that gibberish? . . .
                    Star charts and rubbish . . .
             Is it alchemy? . . .
                    Cheap trickery . . .
             Who is this one with power? . . .

Even if he comes
                Just another trickster.

MEPH.   There they are, whispering,
                        Nit-picking,
                Doubting that the treasure's found.
                One drivels about mandrakes
                Another about the black hound,
                One is sarcastic
                One gets hysterical
                        About magic;
                But you all feel the presence
                Of eternal nature's power;
                You sense
                        A vital force
                Wriggling up from the lower
                        Regions.
                So when you get an itch
                        In your foot,
                A twitch
                        In your leg,
                A tingle up your back,
                When a spot
                Gives you goose bumps:
                Dig! Hack!
                        That's the hole
                Where Nick the fiddler
                        Dumps
                His treasure.

THE CROWD   (*Murmuring*.)
                My big toe's itchy . . .
                        That's gout . . .
                My feet are heavy
                        As lead . . .
                My arm's aching ..
                My back's breaking . . .
                My head's spinning . . .
                I can't hold
                        On, I'm falling . . .
                According to these symptoms
                        This hall
                Must be built on gold.

EMPEROR   If you tell
                   The truth,
               I'll put down sceptre and sword
               And get the royal hands dirty;
               But if there is no hoard,
               I'll send you down you hell.

MEPH.   I think I'll just about
                   Find the way.

EMPEROR   Let's dig it out,
                   Now,
               No delay.

ASTROLOGER   (*Prompted, as before.*)
               Sire, be moderate,
                   Wait;
               First, let the spectacle of colour and love,
                   The carnival, pass.
               We must compose the soul
                   To gain our goal;
               We only win what lies below
                   With help from up above.

EMPEROR   Right. Let's celebrate
               The mad show
                   Of our carnival.

               Trumpets. Exeunt.

MEPH.   Fools never think
                   There is a link
               Between
                   Merit and luck;
               If they had the philosopher's stone
                   They'd still be stuck,
               They'd have no philosopher
                   To use it.

I. 3   Spacious Hall.

*With adjoining rooms, decorated and adorned for the
masquerade.*

HERALD   Don't worry,
                    This isn't going to be
                                German doom and gloom
                    And death dancing;
                    The masquerade
                                Is made
                    In sunny Italy,
                    A steamy festival
                                Awaits you all . . .
                    And I see the crowd
                                begin to grow
                    And swirl;
                                The shy blush and go,
                    The brazen pair off
                                With boy or girl . . .
                    Please don't hesitate
                                To come or go,
                    Early or late . . .
                    The world itself will always be
                                The biggest fool
                    That you can see;
                                Mankind gets its kicks
                    From a million antics.

FEAR   FEAR says:
                    The carnival is full of menace,
                    I am chained within
                                The phantasmagorical furnace;
                    Get away from me,
                                You grinning, ludicrous
                    Revellers;
                    That friend is now my enemy,
                                I know the grin of his murderous
                    Mask, the swish of his evil cape;
                    If only I could escape,
                                Anywhere, any direction;
                    But what's beyond the horizon?
                                Horror and destruction.

HOPE   HOPE says: come to me

My dear sisters;
Today you are masked
But tomorrow I will see
Your sweet faces;
The torchlight and the shadows
Might
Frighten us now,
But soon we will be
Living a carefree
Life in the sunlight,
Strolling in the meadows.

PRUDENCE   Look, two
Of man's great enemies in chains,
FEAR and HOPE;
Don't worry, PRUDENCE
Keeps them away from you.
And look,
I lead
The great Colossus
Carrying a tower,
And on top of the tower
The splendour,
The radiant power
Of the great goddess;
She is VICTORY,
Goddess of glory,
Goddess of success.

DRUNKARD   I feel so frank and frankly I feel free
And I drink:
Clinkity clinkity
Clinty tink
You back there come here
Have a drink.

My little wife she shouted, shouted at me
'Cos I drink:
Clinkity clink clink
Clickerty, tickity
Clunk
Let's all put on masks
'N' get drunk.

Don't tell me I'm confused you'll confuse me
Have a drink:
> Clunk tonk conk kink
> Don't be a bore
> Have a tink clink
> Little drink.
I can't stand up any more.

HERALD   Can't you see it,
A magnificent
> Chariot,
Swerving through the crowd?
But it's not
> Dividing them,
Something's not right:
It passes over the crowd
Like a picture
> From a magic lantern,
A flickering cloud
> Of light.
Suddenly with the thunder
> Of a storm
It's nearly here;
Make way, make way,
> I shudder
With fear.

The chariot arrives. On it are FAUST *as*
PLUTUS, *a* BOY CHARIOTEER, STARVE-
LING, MEANNESS *and* MEPHISTOPHELES.

BOY CHARIOTEER
Stop.

HERALD   Who are you?

BOY CHARIOTEER
We're all allegories;
> You're a herald,
You should know our stories.

HERALD   Forgive me, but I am
> At a loss:
You're not on the carnival programme.
> Who are you, then?

BOY CHARIOTEER
        This is the god
                Most worshipped by men,
        To whom they sacrifice
                Their sanity, their families,
        Their health,
        He whom the Emperor needs
                So urgently:
        PLUTUS, the god of wealth.
        I, too, am immensely rich,
                In my eyes
        I am an equal to the god;
        My name is POETRY.

HERALD
        Surprise
                Us, then
        With your powers.

BOY CHARIOTEER
        Fingers snap, showers
        Of jewels
                Fall sparkling
        To the ground;
                Pearl earrings,
        Exquisite stones
                In priceless rings,
        Diamond combs
                And necklaces;
        And fire
                Set around
        The jewels,
        Ready to flare
                In people's faces.

HERALD
        He flicks the gifts
                To the grasping
        Crowd;
        Jewels stream
                through the air
        As if in a dream;
        But loud
                Dismay:
        Diamonds decay
                Into putty;

Necklaces of pearls
Change into beetles;
The jewels
Are insects
Buzzing round their heads;
The dream of riches dies,
Hard jewels become
Fluttering butterflies.

PLUTUS   If the trick you have done
Has to be defended,
I will tell everyone
You are spirit of my spirit,
You are my dear son.

CHATTERING WOMEN
That's a charlatan
Up there:
Pull him down.
Oh! There's a clown
Hiding behind him,
A village idiot,
A STARVELING
Sick from hunger.

STARVELING   My name
Was once
Dame AVARICE;
Housekeeping
Was my obsession;
Nowadays it's called a vice,
Counting the pennies,
Keeping things nice
And tight
And polished up bright;
Yes, hear me, husbands? *Nowadays*
That's not the fashion;
Housewives give way to passion;
They spend the household finance on
Love and sin;
Their husband's money goes
To Casanovas;
Therefore, I,
Always miserly,

Have changed my sex;
AVARICE now is masculine,
    Making money
From your wives' adultery.

LEADER OF THE WOMEN
    Let dragons
        Breathe on dragons;
    This chariot is full of tricks,
        Cons and put-ons,
    Done to incite
        Boring men
    To fight.

WOMEN ALL TOGETHER
    Scarecrow of sticks,
        Blasphemous crucifix,
    Give him a good
        Couple of kicks
    And he'll splinter,
    This dragon's a bit
        Of old painted wood.

PLUTUS   (*To the* BOY CHARIOTEER.)
    You should not be here,
        In this wild and gaudy company;
    Nor should you be
        Bound to serve money.
    Leave for your natural sphere:
    You belong
    To solitude, to clarity,
        Where you can be
    True to yourself,
    As you sing your song
        Of the world.

BOY CHARIOTEER
    You are my
        Close relative:
    In the ridiculous contest
        mankind has to live,
    People ask which
        Is best?
    A life with you

                              Or a life with me?
              Your followers rest
                              In idleness,
              Mine are poor but busy;
              You are gagged
                              By secrecy;
              But I am free,
                              I only have to breathe
              For everyone to know me.
              Goodbye, then,
                              I know you don't envy
              Me my freedom,.
              And if you want me
                              Whisper softly,
              I'll come
                              Back at once,
              Day or night,
                              If the money's right.

              He goes as he came.

PLUTUS   Look! In iron cauldrons
              The golden blood is boiling,
                              Liquid worth millions;
              It's whirled
                              Round and round,
              In it is forming,
                              Melting and remoulding,
              All the golden jewellery of the world.

THE CROWD   Treasure chests bulge and flow over . . .
              We are all in the clover . . .
                              Gold joins
              The melting pot . . .
                              . . . Look, coins
              Jingle-jangle in streams,
              Pinging on the floor . . .
              I am looking at all my dreams,
              Looking at what my heart
                              Bleeds for . . .
              Where all be rich
              Where all make it . . .
              Dip your hand in and take it . . .

HERALD

You fools make me sick,
      This is just a carnival trick.
You beggar belief,
Don't you know false from true,
      Reality
From trickery?
What makes you think
Gold would be thrown away
On the likes of you?
Masked Plutus,
      Hero of disguises,
Give us some relief,
      Get rid of this rabble for us!

PLUTUS

Give me your rod,
      I'll dip it
Into the molten liquid;
Masks,
      Take care;
See,
How it flashes,
      Sparks
Fly in the air;
Now I come, godly and processional
Among you,
      Careful or you'll be
A bonfire at your funeral.

CROWD

(*Screaming and pushing.*)
We're done for . . .
The fire's in my face . . .
Get back, masks
Get out of the place
      Now! . . .

MEANNESS

I am horribly randy
      With all these women handy;
But with this row
      They can't hear me.
No worry, sneaky
Meanness always finds a way:
Money today is free,
I'll use the money like a lump of clay
      To make a model

In a rude position,
                So all the girls will know
The nature of my proposition.

HERALD   The skinny idiot
                Is kneading
All the gold into a dough;
He squeezes
                A shapeless
Horrible thing, he flicks it
                To the women;
They find it
                Totally repulsive,
They won't give it
                The time of day;
This joker's evil,
                Utterly intolerable,
Give me my rod
                To drive him away.

PLUTUS   No need
                To stop his nonsense,
There's no reaching
                Such a fool;
He does not heed
                The iron rule
That necessity is stronger
Than any moral teaching.

NYMPHS *in chorus, circling* PAN *who is played by the* EMPEROR.

NYMPHS   Here comes the great God Pan,
The cosmic force
                Of life;
He can be coarse
                And grumpy;
But have no fear,
                Be blithe,
Join the lithe
                Dance,
He wants us to be merry;
So honour to you
                Who brought him here.

PLUTUS   (*To the* HERALD.)
                      Whatever happens next,
                              Do nothing
                      And don't worry:
                              Write it all down,
                      The text
                              Will astound posterity.

                      The HERALD *scribbles notes.*

HERALD   And now they lead Great Pan
                      To the fiery fountain;
                      He looks within
                      The hot abyss;
                      But with a pop
                      A flame flares up;
                      Everything turns
                      Chaotic;
                      The Emperor's beard burns,
                      All of him is
                      Pyrotechnic:
                      His flesh boils with a hiss;
                      His companions run
                      To help;
                      But the fire's having fun
                      It makes them yelp
                      With fright
                      And burst alight.
                      They claimed to rule
                      But neglected their tasks,
                      Preferring to play the fool
                      Dressed up in masks;
                      And so they meet their ends
                      In the fire's hot breath,
                      The Emperor's friends:
                      All of them burnt to death.
                      Can a prince
                      Learn from experience?
                      Can the young
                      Curb their exuberance?
                      And now the crown
                      Itself melts down,
                      The flames leap
                      Across the country;

Is this the fate
Of the imperial state,
To be
A smouldering ash-heap?

PLUTUS   Enough of fire;
                        Fog and mists
                Dampen the panic,
                Rain
                        Wash away
                The pain,
                Tame
                        The frightening
                Flame;
                Make the fires
                        Harmless summer lightning.
                When demons come out for a ride
                We need magic on our side.

I. 4   Pleasure Garden

Morning sun. The EMPEROR *is waving people to get up.*

FAUST   Do you forgive
                        Our fiery illusions, Sire?

EMPEROR   Suddenly I was Pluto
                        In a glowing sphere,
                Spinning in the air;
                A rocky valley
                        Was beneath me;
                Then fire flickered up
                        And I was suspended
                In a vast dome,
                Attended
                        By thousands who paid
                Homage to me
                        From the flames;
                I knew the names
                        Of some, my courtiers;
                It seemed I was
                        Lord of the salamanders.

MEPH.   And so you are, Sire!
                         All the elements
               Recognize the might of your majesty,
               Even fire
                         Is your subject;
               Your powers reign
                         unconditionally;
               Please, eject
                         Your imperial self
               From the window
                         Into the roaring sea below;
               As you leap
                         The royal health
               Will be safe;
                         A sphere of space
               Will enfold you
                         All your wealth
               Will follow you,
               Streaming
                         Like arrows
               Of light into the dark
               Depths of the ocean;
               The great monsters of the deep
                         Will peep
               Into your palace windows;
               You will laugh
                         Into the gaping
               Mouth of the mighty shark.

EMPEROR   What favourable fate
                         Brought you to me, straight
               Out of the Arabian Nights?
               If your flights
                         Of fancy
               Are as full as frenzy
                         As those of Scheherazade,
               You'll be the royal favourite.
               Always be ready;
                         The hard
               World of the day
                         Revolts me.

SENESCHAL   (*Entering in haste.*)
               Your majesty,

A miracle;
The national debt's
            Been swept away;
The creditor withdraws his claws
From the nation's throat;
A groat
            Is worth a groat again.
Who needs the thrills
Of paradise?
            We can pay
Off all the bills!

COMMANDER-IN-CHIEF

All the back pay's paid;
            The army gains
Recruits everyday,
New blood runs in the veins
            Of the mercenary,
The whores and the landlords rub
            Their hands;
Soldiers are spending in every pub.

TREASURER   (*Joining the others.*)
Ask who did the miracle.

CHANCELLOR   This is the fateful
            Piece of paper,
That changed pain to gain
            And spurious happiness:

He reads.

'This paper
            Is worth a thousand crowns;
That worth
            Is guaranteed;
Redeemable against
The Emperor's gold
            Buried in the earth.'

EMPEROR   This is a terrible crime. I cannot endure
            Fraud on such a scale.
Well? Do we know who forged
            The imperial signature?

TREASURER   But you signed it,
                          Last night.
                 You were dressed up as
                          The great God Pan;
                 The Chancellor said
                 'Now you can
                          Give the people
                 Immeasurable pleasure
                 With the stroke of a pen.'
                          Then,
                 That very night,
                          Thousands and thousands of notes
                 Were copied and printed;
                 Now everything in the garden's
                          Sunny,
                 Suddenly everyone finds
                          Everything very funny,
                 It's the perfect kind of money.

EMPEROR   And are my people really happy,
                          With paper rather than gold?
                 Courtiers, soldiers, landlords
                          Even whores?
                 Well, I suppose I must believe
                          What I am told.

TREASURER   The Chancellor and the criminals
                          Are far away;
                 The banks are open;
                          They honour the bits of paper
                 With gold and silver,
                          Though, of course,
                 With a cut for commission;
                 The takers
                          Of easy money hasten
                 To the butchers and the bakers,
                          The vintners and the tailors,
                 Then back to the bank again:
                 The nation
                          Is at an orgy
                 Of spending, drinking
                 'Here's a health to his majesty
                          And his pen.'

FAUST   Fantastical money,
                    Based on frozen wealth
        Which no one can handle,
                    No one can see,
        Of such immensity
                    It defeats
        The loftiest imagination;
        Yet minds with the courage
                    To think deeply,
        Unafraid of infinity,
                    May grasp the mystery.

MEPH.   Such bits of paper
                    Are practical economics;
        Why deal with the market
                    And exchange,
        Why budget and rave
                    About having to save?
        Ignore the sceptics;
        It's fine
                    To spend what you've not got;
        You can have the lot,
        All of the love and all of the wine.

EMPEROR   And our empire shows
                    Its gratitude;
        We entrust to you
                    The Imperial underground;
        You are the curators
                    Of the treasure that glows
        Below;
        Only on your orders
                    Will the hoard be excavated.
        Treasurers,
                    Enjoy your elevated
        Rank;
        By this happy policy
                    Upperworld
        And underworld
                    Are, at once, united.

TREASURER   Delighted to make
                    An admission:

I've always wanted
> To work with a magician.

Exits.

EMPEROR   A bag of plenty of money
> To anyone
Who says what they want
To spend it on.

Exits.

PAGE   (*Receiving.*)
I want to spend it on being me,
> And happy.

ANOTHER   (*Likewise.*)
I want to give my girl things;
> The usual:
Necklaces, rings . . .

CHAMBERLAIN
> (*Accepting.*)
I'll use mine
>> To double what I spend on wine.

ANOTHER   (*Likewise.*)
I'll put good hard
> Cash
On the turn of a card.

STANDARD-BEARER
> (*Thoughtfully.*)
I'll get
>> My land and castle out of debt.

ANOTHER   (*Likewise.*)
I want the money . . .
> To put with my other money.

FAUST   (*To* MEPHISTOPHELES.)
I had hoped to hear
> Of desire for a better life,
Hoped to have seen

        Courage and great deeds;
But now I know you all too well;
You are what you've always been.

FOOL   You're giving away
                Money, fine:
So where's mine?

FAUST   Ah, the old fool;
                You'll follow the drunk's
Golden rule,
What you have today, drink away.

FOOL   The magical bank notes;
                Is this a kind of money
That floats?

FAUST   Only a fool
                Gloats over money.

FOOL   But it is floating,
                The notes are fluttering
About, more and more,
                In and out of doors,
In the roads, over roofs,
In the guttering . . .

FAUST   Just take them, they're all yours!

        Exit.

FOOL   'Scuse me,
                Could I have five million crowns?

MEPH.   I can't stand dead clowns
                Who come back to life.

FOOL   That kind of thing happens to me,
                But not as wonderfully
As this.

MEPH.   You say you're happy, yet
                You've broken out in a sweat.

FOOL

It's the money. Is this its true
    Value?

MEPH.

You can buy
    All that you can pour
Down your throat into you belly.

FOOL

Can I buy a house, animals, land?

MEPH.

Just hold out your hand.
    I'd love to see the likes of you
As Lord of a manor.

FOOL

Tonight I'll be
    A property owner!

Exit.

MEPH.

Oh well,
    A fool's paid to be funny;
You can't deny him
    Funny money.

I. 5   A Gloomy Gallery

FAUST *and* MEPHISTOPHELES.

MEPH.

What is this fit
    Of melancholy?
Why drag me to these gloomy
    Corridors?
Isn't the opportunity
    For tricks and whispers,
Amongst the crowd of couriers,
Fun enough for you?

FAUST

You've talked too much like that.
    You used to wear
Out the soles of your shoes
    Running everywhere,
At my service;
Now you only rush about

To avoid me.
But now I'm been pressured
            By the Chamberlain
To perform for the Emperor again;
I promised his majesty he'd see
            Helen of Troy and Paris;
The image of the ideal;
So get to work.
            He wants them now
And he wants them to be real.

MEPH.   A stupid promise. Do you think
                    I can do that
                At the drop of a hat,
                    Any-old-how?

FAUST   You've not thought, my friend,
                    Where your tricks will end;
                Because we made him
                    Rich beyond imagination,
                He thinks we can supply
                    Endless fun and titillation.

MEPH.   You think Helen can be conjured up
                    As easily
                As the spectre of paper money?
                Now, a pubescent witch,
                A lecherous ghost
                    Or a ghoulish girl
                With a sexy goitre,
                The Devil's sweethearts
                    Who loiter
                On dark corners,
                I'll drum them up for you
                    Anytime;
                But to summon the sublime
                    Helen,
                Greek heroine, the glory
                Of phantoms, that needs a pagan spell;
                    Pagan affairs
                Inhabit an entirely
                    Different kind of hell.
                But there may
                    Be a way.

FAUST   Tell me.

MEPH.   There are others
                        Involved.

FAUST   Others?

MEPH.   (*Whispers*.)
               They are called The Mothers.

FAUST   There's something strange
               In the way you say
                        their name.
               Who are they?

MEPH.   Goddesses,
                        Beyond the range
               Of mortal comprehension.
               You have to know how
                        To journey down
               Deep within to find them;
                        And all because
               Of your reckless promises.

FAUST   Where is the path?

MEPH.   There is no path.
               Are you ready
                        To do what cannot be done?
               For we must tread
                        Where none has trod;
               Enter
                        Where none has entered;
               We must win
                        What cannot be won,
               Ask what cannot be asked.
               There are no locks
                        To unlock,
               No bolts
                        To slide aside;
               Nowhere to go,
                        Nowhere to hide;
               You must survive

The loneliness of isolation,
The pit of desolation.

FAUST

I've had the pick
     Of speeches like that
From you:
     Witches' kitchen rhetoric.
Come on!
We got through
     That mumbo-jumbo
Years ago:
I know the isolation
     Of futile study;
As for the pit
     Of desolation,
I learnt the meaning of emptiness,
Then I taught it!
When I proposed a new
     Kind of reason,
What did I receive?
     Mindless derision.
I had to flee
     From my colleagues' calumny,
I was hurled
Into a wilderness
     Of rejection;
I learnt the cruel way of the world;
With no position, fortune or friend,
     In order not to live a life
Of poverty, wasted
     By intellectual strife,
In the end I . . .
     Yes, in the end
I gave myself to the Devil.

MEPHISTOPHELES *bows.*

MEPH.

But even if you swam
     Against the motions
Of the mighty tides
     Of all the oceans
Even if you
     Were in terror

Of your immediate death
You'd still see something:
Dolphins gliding in the green water,
   Clouds shifting
Shapes above you,
   The sun, the moon, the stars
Of starlight . . .
But in the endless
   Empty distance
In the final emptiness
   You'll not hear your footfall;
You will be
   In freefall.

FAUST   What do you want to do,
       Mephisto?
    Make me go
       Into that void
    To help you?
    To pick a chestnut
       Out of the fire for you?
    Or to finally curse
       Me?
    Fine. I consent.
    I believe
       In reckless experiment.
    For in your void I hope to find
       The universe.

MEPH.   Before you go,
       I have to say
    That in a way
       You do impress me;
    You are a true
       scholar;
    You've learnt the ways of hell
    Very well.
    Here, take
       This key.

FAUST   That tiny thing?

MEPH.   Don't underestimate
       It.

FAUST   It's starting to vibrate,
                    It glows . . .

MEPH.   Follow
                    What it opens,
             Below
                    To the Mothers.

FAUST   A beautiful word, 'Mothers',
             That the mind knows
                    Is comforting;
                    What, then, shudders
             My soul?

MEPH.   If a mere word
                    Shudders your 'soul',
             You've got a whole
             Set of problems ahead.
                    Nothing should bother you;
             No words, no talk;
             You are a living man
                    Who's seen the dead walk.

FAUST   True,
                    I've seen so much,
             Thanks to you.
             But I don't seek salvation
                    In cold calculation;
             Man's best feature
                    Is the capacity
             To control fear;
             Whatever the world demands
                    In recompense,
             The man who feels truly
                    Can know the immense.

MEPH.   Then sink, or rise;
                    Up, down;
             Is it a surprise
                    To know that they're the same?
             Do you dare to play the eternal game:
             Enter the sphere
                    Of ideological shapes;
             Delight in escapes

From the prison of ideas
That long ago ceased to exist?
Systems of belief
            Are as brief
As clouds weaving and reforming;
            Will you swing the key,
Turn it in nothing
            And flee?

FAUST   (*Enthusiastic.*)
Yes, I feel a new strength,
            I take a deep breath,
I am ready for flight
            And fall,
Great height and terrible depth.

MEPH.   Deeper than those higher
            Depths,
You will find
A tripod,
            In it a fire,
In the flames of the fire
You will see
            The Mothers:
Some moving, some still,
Some in a transformation
            Beyond imagination,
Surrounded by floating
            Images of creation;
They won't see you,
            They are a shadow
Of a greater reality;
But now be
            Brave,
There is great danger;
            Go to the tripod
And touch it with the key.

FAUST *makes a decisive, commanding
gesture with the key.*

MEPH.   (*Watching him.*)
That's right.
            The tripod will come alive,

It will be your slave;
                In a flash
You dash
                Back here with it
And thrive;
By a chemical-magical formula
With the tripod's incense
You can call
                All the heroines of antiquity
Quickly
                Straight into the Emperor's hall.

FAUST   Good. So now I . . .

MEPH.   Strive,
                With your whole
Sense of being alive,
Ever upwards, to go down;
Climb a mountain
                That's a great big hole.

FAUST *stamps his foot and sinks away.*

MEPH.   Mm. Will he
                Freeze or burn,
Or use his key
                And return?

I. 6   Imperial Palace: Brightly Lit Halls

EMPEROR *and* PRINCES. *Bustle of the court.*

CHAMBERLAIN (*To* MEPHISTOPHELES.)
                When
                Will you give us the scene
With the ghost of Helen?
Get to work, the Emperor
                Is impatient.

SENESCHAL   And you don't want
                An impatient Emperor.

MEPH.   That is why my colleague went;
                     He's locked himself away;
             He needs to be apart;
             To raise
                     The greatest beauty of the ages
             Requires
             Concentration and the highest art:
                     The magic of the sages.

SENESCHAL   Never mind the art;
                     The Emperor says start.

BLONDE   (*To* MEPHISTOPHELES.)
             A word sir,
                     Have you got a cure
             For freckles?
             They come out all over
                     In the summer.

MEPH.   Ah, Summer speckles,
                     Dotted like a tabby cat.
             Take an extract
                     Of toad-tongue,
             Boil with frog spawn
             At dawn,
                     And spread upon your skin
             When the moon is thin
                     And waning.

BRUNETTE   My foot is frozen;
                     I am lame;
             I can't join in the game
             Of flirting and dancing:
                     I'm even clumsy
             When I curtsey.

MEPH.   Allow me
             To play footsie,
                     To give you
             A good kick with my foot.

BRUNETTE   But that's what lovers do.

MEPH.   My kick has a deeper meaning,

> Like to like,
> Foot healing
> > Foot.
> Please lift you skirts.

BRUNETTE   Ow, that hurts!
> > A kick like a horse's hoof.

MEPH.   But the kick of a beast
> > Has cured you.
> Off you go,
> Dance with your lovers at the feast.

LADY   (*Pressing forward.*)
> I've pains
> Destroying me
> > All over,
> It's jealousy;
> 'Til yesterday he saw salvation in my eyes;
> > Now he lies,
> He slips
> > Away to her, gossips
> With her, and turns his back on me.

MEPH.   Alarming, but use a little bit of art:
> > Sneak up on your lover,
> With this bit of coal;
> > Draw
> A line, down shoulder
> > Arm and sleeve;
> Remorse will sink
> > A knife into his heart;
> Eat the coal, drink
> No wine or water,
> And he'll be there,
> > Slobbering at your door.

LADY   You're not telling me to take
> > Poison?

MEPH.   (*Indignantly.*)
> Lady, this piece of coal
> > Came from a burning
> At the stake;

>Could there be a greater guarantee
>Of purity?

PAGE

>I want to be in love,
>   But no one
>Takes me seriously.

MEPH.

>(*Aside*.)
>I don't know who
>   To listen to:
>This is beginning to rattle me.

To the PAGE.

>Son,
>   Forget the young.
>Go for older women,
>   They're willing and a lot more fun.

OTHERS *are pressing forward.*

>More and more,
>   What a battle,
>I'm in trouble;
>   The hooved one's being forced
>To make up magic
>   On the hoof!
>It's tragic:
>   I'll have to be really low,
>And use the worst trick of all:
>   Telling the truth.
>Oh Mothers, Mothers,
>   Let Faust go!

I. 7   The Knight's Hall

Subdued lighting. The EMPEROR *and the Court have taken their places.*

MEPH.

>The Master has spoken:
>   Start the play;
>Walls, open!

And tapestries dissolve
To nothing;
  The walls revolve
And to the low rumble
  Of a gigantic drum,
A deep theatre
  Forms,
Lit by mysterious light.
Now I'll climb up
  To the proscenium.

Emerging from the prompt-box.

From here I perform my part
  Of prompter,
To general approval;
After all,
  Prompting is the Devil's art.

ASTROLOGER By magic powers,
  See an example
Of a mighty ancient temple.

ARCHITECT Over-rated, out of date:
The crude is called noble,
  The awkward called great.
As an architect
  I celebrate
Slender pillars rising
  To infinity,
Designed
  To edify the mind.

FAUST (*Majestically.*)
I do this in your names,
  You who live
Alone yet together
  In one place but no place,
In the dark of endless space.
Images of life
  Now lifeless,
Float around your heads;
But a life that once glowed with glory
  Stirs,

Desperate for eternity;
It's you who have the right
      To send it on its way
To the bright pavilions of day
      Or the dark vaults of night.

ASTROLOGER   The glowing key
      Touches the bowl;
Fog rises
      To clog
The room with gloom,
      The mist
Thins,
      A veil hangs
In the air,
And suddenly
A beautiful youth
      Strolls towards us:
PARIS.

LADY   So young, so strong
      And his legs, so long . . .

SECOND LADY   A peach,
      Gobble him up . . .

THIRD LADY   Reach
      Out to those lips . . .

FOURTH LADY   What I'd give
      For a few sips
From his cup . . .

FIFTH LADY   Pretty,
      Though not refined . . .

SIXTH LADY   Do we mind?
      Though there is something
Of the peasant
      Present . . .

KNIGHT   A shepherd,
      Not a prince of Troy;
This is a country boy.

ANOTHER KNIGHT
                    He looks fit;
                            But that may be a lot
                    Of fancy muscle; kit
                            Him up in armour
                    And see what we've got.

LADY   He's sitting down,
                            What slow
                    Languor,
                    Almost feminine.

KNIGHT   Maybe you want to hang your
                            Head on his lap . . .

ANOTHER LADY
                    He's flicked off a sandal;
                            He's bent his arm
                    Behind his head . . .
                    Do you think he wants to go to bed?

CHAMBERLAIN
                    How uncouth.
                            This is a scandal.

LADY   You men have to criticise.

CHAMBERLAIN
                    He lies
                            There, lolling! Lolling
                    Before the Emperor!

LADY   He's an actor,
                            Acting that he's alone.

CHAMBERLAIN
                    The play should have
                            A more elevated, courtly tone.

LADY   Now the pretty boy is sleeping.

CHAMBERLAIN
                    And snoring.
                            How disgustingly natural.

YOUNG LADY   (*Delighted.*)
                  What's that new scent, mingling
                              With the incense,
                  Refreshing me
                              So deeply?

OLDER LADY   I have it too, a scent
                  That's light with flowers
                              But dim
                  With musk;
                              That enters
                  My very soul . . .
                  I think it comes from him.

OLDEST LADY   It is the fresh
                              Smell of youth,
                  Of flesh
                  Made of Ambrosia,
                              Transforming the air
                  Around him.

                  HELEN *enters.*

MEPH.   Here she is, then;
                              The famous Helen,
                  From the oldest story ever told.
                  Quite pretty;
                              Frankly, though,
                  She leaves me cold.

FAUST   Is it something other than
                              The evidence of our eyes
                  That lets us see
                              Shining beauty;
                  Is there a source
                              Deep within my soul,
                  From which it pours
                              So abundantly?
                  Now I know
                  My dangerous journey
                              Has brought a great reward.
                  How dull the world
                              Seemed before,
                  Closed and unexplored;

But, with this priesthood,
My old world is past,
My new one delights,
The vision will last
Forever.
May my breath
Stop, should I ever
Tire of you;
The image of you
I loved in the magic mirror
Was an error,
A distorted reflection
Of your true beauty;
I pledge to you
All the passion,
The affection,
The frenzy
The insanity
Of the heart.

MEPH.   (*From the prompt-box.*)
Please calm yourself down
And stick to your part.

OLDER LADY   Tall,
Good figure,
But her head's too small.

YOUNGER LADY
Her feet are flat.

DIPLOMAT   I think she's a princess,
Worthy of a crown;
Beautiful, all the way up
And all the way down.

COURTIER   She's sneaking over
To the sleeper,
Softly . . .

LADY   Doesn't she look ugly
Compared to him.

POET   On the contrary,

                    She is illuminated
        By his beauty.

LADY   Endymion and the moon:
                    It's like a painting!

POET   Yes, his pose
                    Slows,
                She sinks
                    And drinks
                A kiss . . .
                If only I could enjoy
                    What makes me so jealous.

DUENNA   In front of everyone,
                    It's outrageous!

FAUST   A fatal kiss for the boy,
                    If I
                Have anything to do with it!

MEPH.   Be quiet, sit
                    Absolutely still.
                Let the phantoms
                    Do what they will.

COURTIER   She breaks
                    From their embrace
                And slips away
                    With light-footed grace;
                He wakes.

LADY   She looks back;
                I knew she would!

COURTIER   He's amazed;
                    It's as if it were
                A miracle.

LADY   It doesn't seem a miracle
                    To her.

COURTIER   She turns to him,
                    With modesty.

LADY   He'll get a burst
                        Of her temper soon;
                Men are so stupid
                        About arrows and cupid;
                Why do they always think
                        They're the first?

KNIGHT   No, she will always be
                        The epitome
                Of refined majesty.

LADY   Don't you think I can
                        Tell a courtesan
                From a lady?
                She's after all the fish in the sea.

PAGE   She can get her hook into me.

PROFESSOR   As a classical professor,
                        I doubt whether
                She is genuine;
                I don't trust
                        The human senses;
                I prefer the written word
                        To personal experiences.
                Though I admit,
                        Despite my age,
                Her presence on the stage
                        Provokes
                An overwhelming lust.

ASTROLOGER   This isn't a boy any more!
                        See him go
                To her, like a real hero;
                His blood
                        Is on fire,
                His arms flood
                        With strength,
                He lifts her
                        From the floor;
                Will he carry her away?

FAUST   Leave her alone! This is
                        Too much,

Put her down, don't dare touch
    Her.

MEPH.   But this is all your work:
    Do you want to smash the glass
Of stage pretence
    And act in your own farce?

PROFESSOR   If this were a book,
    I'd look
For a title something like:
'The Minds of Men
    And The Rape Of Helen.'

FAUST   What rape?
    Am I not here to shape
The reality before me?
Isn't this key
    In my hand?
It led me
Through terror,
The surge of waves in a sea
    Of desolation,
To firm land,
And here I stand:
    Here the spirit
Fights against phantoms;
Here the realm of fantasy
    Becomes
Reality.
I'll save her, she'll be doubly mine;
I'll be her maker and her lover;
I'll risk it!
    Mothers, allow
It! How,
Having once seen her,
    Could I ever leave her?

ASTROLOGER   Faust, Faust!
    What's come over him?
He clutches
    Her,
The image of Helen goes dim;
He turns the key toward the boy

                             He touches
                Him . . . Oh! Oh!

                Explosion, FAUST *lying on the floor. The*
                SPIRITS *dissolve into a haze.*

MEPH.   (*Taking* FAUST *on his shoulder.*)
                So typical.
                             Make a friend
                Of a fool,
                And Even the Devil
                             Suffers in the end.
Darkness. Commotion.

ACT TWO

II. 1   High-Vaulted, Narrow Gothic Chamber

Formerly FAUST'*s, unchanged.*

MEPH.   Yes lie there, a demented wreck,
                             Caught in the snare
                Of a hopeless love affair;
                If you've been paralysed
                             By the poison of loving Helen
                You'll not regain your reason
                             Easily.

                He looks around.

                Hallowed
                             Territory,
                Faust's old study;
                The light
                             Through the stain glass
                Is dimmer;
                Deft
                             Spiders' webs
                Drift over the books;

The paper has yellowed,
The ink has dried;
But everything still looks
As it was the night
            He left;
There's the quill,
With which the Doctor
Signed himself away
            To the devil:
Yes,
There on the nib,
            A spot, a little clot
Of blood,
Which I made seep
            From his veins.
These relics are unique,
Enough to make
            An antique dealer weep.

And the fur of his academic gown
Still hangs on the back of the door;
It reminds me of all the high-blown
            Nonsense I once fed
Into the poor, credulous head
Of a student I used to know;
No doubt he's spewing it all back out
            To others even now.
I'm sorely-tempted to dress up, to be
The trumped-up, puffed-up professor again,
            Convinced of his infallibility.
The professors know
            How to always be in the right;
The Devil gave up that particular fight
            A long, long time ago.

*He takes the fur gown off the hook and shakes
it; crickets, beetles and moths fall out.*

Insects, beetles, creepy-crawlies
Quick, quick,
            Jump, creak, click,
Hide in a hundred thousand
            Nooks and crannies.

Putting the gown on.

The fall of black silk
            Over my shoulders;
Ah to be a university
            Don again, curdling the milk
Of youth.
But the new generations don't care;
            My words leave them cold,
The young can be very dim.
Never mind:
            Remember, the Devil is old,
And only the old
            Understand him.

*He pulls the bell which sounds with a shrill
piercing tone so that the rooms vibrate and the
doors fly open.*

MEPH.   Who wouldn't know at once
            The noble Doctor Wagner,
Pupil of Faust, not at all a dunce,
On the contrary, now the first,
            The most senior
Scholar in academia;
He, alone, continues the research;
Science is his church:
Like a monk of the intellect
            He locks himself away
In solitude.
This refined man of learning
            Looks like a crude
Back-woodsman,
            Blackened by charcoal burning
From ears to nose,
Eyes red from the way he blows
            At the fire.

MEPHISTOPHELES *moves his castor-chair
nearer to the proscenium. He speaks to the
audience.*

It's dark up here, fetid, not air;
I think I'll sit with you down there.

II. 2   Laboratory

In the style of the Middle Ages; extensive apparatus, for fantastical purposes.

WAGNER	(*At the furnace.*)
	Please, someone stop that bell
	It will break
	My concentration;
	The solemn expectation
	Is utterly unbearable;
	Can I tell
	The world that after
	All the years of experimentation
	I can make
	The great unmakable?
	Deep within the phial I can see
	Something that grows; it glows
	Like a blood-red ruby;
	It radiates flashing light;
	At last, if I can get it right
	This time . . . Oh the door, who is it?
MEPH.	(*Entering.*)
	Good evening. Please, this is no more
	Than a courtesy visit.
WAGNER	Please! Observe absolute silence.
	You come at a great moment for science.
MEPH.	Why, what are you doing?
WAGNER	I am making a human being.
MEPH.	Really? Please tell the class
	How you hope to do that:
	Have you got two lovers
	Doing the deed of darkness
	In your furnace?
WAGNER	God forbid. The old way of birth is a farce.
	We need another method of propagation,
	That protects the feeble moment of creation,
	That helps the power of life

In its struggle to gain its strengths;
Enjoyable though they be, the ludicrous lengths
That the beasts have to indulge in
In order to have children,
Are undignified for Man;
In the future we can
Be truer to our higher origin.

Turning to the furnace.

The preparation begins to clear,
The great moment draws near.
I am happy in my certainty;
What used to be a holy mystery
Now we can harness rationally;
What forces of nature organically organise,
We can artificially crystallise.

MEPH. I've lived too long,
                Nothing's a surprise;
I've seen many artificial people crystallise.

WAGNER *has been watching the phial
carefully.*

WAGNER It rises to the apogee
Of its accumulation;
Any moment now it will achieve
Auto-fertilisation.
A great advance seems crazy in its day;
But the future won't conceive
Of human birth in any other way;
Nothing will be left to the vagaries
Of the mating of random personalities;
The brain of a brilliant thinker
Will father a brilliant thinker.

Looking at the phial in delight.

The glass clears, it cools 'til it's merely warm;
And through the glass I see the delicate form
Of a little man, a man-manikin; did he move?
Now we have what the world wanted: we'll
                                    rejoice,

The mystery of life is within our power; listen,
A sound in the phial; the vital signs quicken;
The sound will become a voice.

HOMUNCULUS (*In the phial, to* WAGNER.)
Alright, Daddikins?
                That was a near
Thing.
            Come,
Give me
            A great, big, slobby
Hug, Daddy dear.
But not so hard
            You break the thin
Glass wall;
If you are part of nature
            The whole of the cosmos
Is too small;
            But the artificial
Needs to be shut in.

To MEPHISTOPHELES.

And you're here too,
You old joker in crime,
My honourable
            Cousin,
Thank you for coming
At such a good time:
While I live
            I must be active;
Work and play!
            Your experience
Will show me the way.

WAGNER   Please I have so many questions, like:
                How are the body and the soul joined together?
                By some kind of spike?
                And why do they want to stay that way
                When, so obviously, they hate each other?
                And . . .

MEPH.   No, I'll ask:
                Why do men and women

> Fight for love,
> Then love to fight?
> You'll never get
> > *That* one right.
> Now, if you don't mind, I have a task,
> Just for a little, like you.

HOMUNCULUS   Anything you want to do.

MEPH.   (*Pointing to a side-door.*)
Show off your genius, then!

WAGNER   (*Still looking at the phial.*)
I do so enjoy
Looking at my lovely boy.

The side-door opens, one can see FAUST
stretched out on the bed.

HOMUNCULUS (*Astonished.*)
A vision.

The phial slips out of WAGNER's *hands and
hovers over* FAUST, *illuminating him.*

> Beautiful landscape,
> > Clear pool of water
> In thick
> > Forest,
> > Lovely women
> Undressed –
> This is terrific –
> One is a true
> > Beauty,
> Clearly descended from heroes
> Or a god's daughter;
> > Her long back
> Curves,
> > She dips her toes
> Into the water,
> The flame of life
> > In her warm skin
> Cools;
> But what has she done that deserves

The sudden roar, the buzzing
And splashing, wrecking
    The water's smooth mirror?
What is this whirring
    Of mighty wings?
The other women run away,
But she's content to stay;
With a sigh
    Of feminine pleasure,
She enjoys
    The princely swan-boy's
Feathery pressure
    On her thigh;
So tame,
    So eager for the game . . .
But suddenly,
    A mist
Falls like a screen,
Obscuring the charming scene.

MEPH.   Though small,
You are an enormous fantasist;
I didn't see
    Anything at all.

HOMUNCULUS Of course not.
    You're from the cold
Germanic north,
    Full of old
Rubbish, monks, teutonic knights;
It's no surprise
    You can't use your eyes:
Your home is in dark forests
Full of gloom and doom.

Looking around.

And look at this room;
    Mildewed walls;
Pointed arches,
    Plaster scrolls,
All in the most vulgar taste;
When he wakes up, faced
With this gothic pigsty

He'll die;
He was full of optimism;
                His dream
Was of classical things,
                Swans and nudes
Bathing in woodland springs;
This was a man with hope,
How could he cope
                With this barbarism?
We
                Must get him away from here.

MEPH.   I very much agree.

HOMUNCULUS Cometh the hour cometh the man,
Cometh the girl
                Cometh the dance,
And all is well:
                With a glance
At my artificial memory,
I see
                That Classical Walpurgis Night
Is happening as we speak;
                There he can unwind
His mind
                In its element.

MEPH.   A *classical* witch's night?
I've never heard of it.

HOMUNCULUS How could you? You sit
Up here, with awful
                Romantic spooks;
But a real ghoul
                Has got to be classical.

MEPH.   Do we really
                Have to go to Greece?
My classical colleagues
                Are so pretentious,
I find them quite nauseous.

HOMUNCULUS Your pleasure playground's
                In Germany, Satan;

But now we sail to the South;
To sweeter sounds
Wafted in sweeter air,
        Where the River Peneus flows
Through lush meadows,
Spreading upon a great plain
        To its mouth
With lush and peaceful coves;
The plain stretches from the sea
        To mountainous ravines,
Where the fabled Pharsalus . . .

MEPH.   That's enough! Oh the pain,
                Endless sagas
                        Of heroes and heroines;
                Endless scenes
                        Of battles against tyranny;
                The brain
                        Caves in;
                They say it's all about freedom;
                Come come,
                        It's just slaves killing slaves.

HOMUNCULUS   Leave humans to their fractious
                        Nature;
                The boy must torture
                Himself to grow into a man.
                Meanwhile, what can
                        We do for this one?

MEPH.   I'd like to have had some fun
                        With lots of little Brocken tricks,
                But Olympian bolts
                        Stop me.
                These Greeks are dolts:
                They dazzle and seduce you with their sensual
                                                        play,
                Enticing the heart away
                        To cheerful sins,
                As if sins could be clean and pretty:
                But we Northerners know sins
                        Must be gloomy and dirty.
                What shall we do now?

HOMUNCULUS Get the cloak you flew
                             Here in;
                    Wrap him up,
                             You in there too;
                    I'll be
                             Light to lead your way.

WAGNER   (*Anxiously.*)
                    What about me?

HOMUNCULUS You stay
                             Home in your study;
                    Translate the contents
                    Of musty,
                             Ancient scrolls;
                    Collect the elements,
                             Analyze each one
                    Meticulously;
                             Contemplate the 'what'
                    And the even trickier 'how';
                    And now
                             I must leave,
                    To wander the world,
                    On a voyage of discovery:
                             I hope to find the dot
                    To put on the i.
                    Bye bye.

WAGNER   (*Sadly.*)
                    Goodbye. There's pain
                    In this farewell.
                    I fear I'll I never see you again,
                    My strange son.

MEPH.   Now, South, down
                             To the Peneus,
                    And quickly;
                    Don't treat your honourable cousin
                             Too lightly.
                    It is the fate
                             Of all of us
                    To depend on creatures we create.

II. 3   Classical Walpurgis-Night: the Pharsalian Fields

Darkness. The travellers in the air, from above.

HOMUNCULUS Fly, looking down
                        At the horror of the inferno,
            The valley and the plain
                        Flickering with flames
            Far below.

MEPH.   I find great consolation
                        Seeing
            Such gruesome ghosts,
            Such horror and desolation:
            It's just like
                        Looking out of the window
            When I'm back home.

HOMUNCULUS Set your man down,
                        He'll revive
            At once;
                        He'll be
            In ecstasy:
            This is all he wants,
            To be alive
                        In a world of fantasy.

FAUST   (*Alone.*)
            Where is she?
                        No need to ask;
            This may not be
                        Her shore,
            Her earth or sea;
            But it is the air
                        That bore
            Her speech.
            I woke from a deep sleep,
                        Inspired;
            I knew at once, by a miracle
                        I was where I desired,
            Above all other places, to be:
            In Greece.
                        So now I stand
            On the land

Of myths and heroes;
I am strong as Antaeus,
And whatever
Dangers I encounter,
I will plunge into
The labyrinth of infernos.

II. 4   On the Upper Peneus

MEPH.   (*Prying around.*)
Wandering round
These little fires,
I feel
Very foreign,
Very out of place;
I'm no prude,
But I find a blush
Even on the Devil's face,
To see so many in the nude:
Do these men think it obscene
To be seen
In a shirt,
Or the women, in a skirt?
The Sphinxes are shameless,
The Griffins
Outrageous;
And all these disreputable
Creatures in curly wigs,
Quite out of their minds
With bare fronts and bare behinds . . .
I mean, one relishes the lewd,
But this antiquity
Is too life-loving;
One needs some modern taste,
Paste
A fig leaf
Here and there,
A fashionable covering
To give us some relief
From this crudity.
A pest
Of a people;

                              Thoroughly disagreeable;
                    Still, I am their guest,
                              I must be civil.
                    Greetings, ladies;
                    Greetings,
                              Ancient sages.

SPHINX   We don't know you,
                              So
                    What's your name?

MEPH.   I have many names.
                              Are there any Britons around?
                    They have a mania for antiquity;
                    Walking the ground
                              Of old battle fields;
                    Staring at scenically pleasing waterfalls,
                    And dreary old ruins
                              With crumbling walls;
                    They'd love it here for their holidays.
                              The Britons have a
                    A name for me,
                              In their old plays;
                    Old Iniquity.

FIRST GRIFFIN (*Croaking.*)
                    This one looks
                              A wrong 'un.

SECOND GRIFFIN
                              A wrong 'un
                              After what?

BOTH   Nasty wrong 'n
                              You don't belong
                    Round here.

MEPH.   (*Violently.*)
                    Do you think your guests'
                              Fingernails
                    Can't slit
                              You from ear to ear,
                    Just because

You've got sharp claws?
Let's try it!

SPHINX (*Mildly.*)
Stay if you like,
            But you'll get homesick,
Nostalgic
            For your country,
Where you take a pride
In really being somebody.

MEPH.   Sphinx, up top
            You look a feast
Of beauty;
But down below
            You are a beast
And filthy.

SPHINX Father of lies,
            You'll bitterly regret that;
Our claws in our paws
            Are healthy;
Your hoof is shrivelled and clumsy;
You're out of place
            In this classical company.

The SIRENS *strike up a prelude from above.*

MEPH.   Who are the birds
            In the branches
Of the poplar trees,
Swaying in the breeze?

SPHINX Take care;
            The noblest man
Cannot resist
            The strong
Seduction of their song.

SIRENS Why be content with fantasy,
And all that's dull and ugly?
Listen, we flock to you,
Singing in harmony;
Come with us and be

Part of our song
And forever happy.

MEPH.   This warbling may be art,
                    But all I hear
             Is a kind of buzzing in my ear;
                    It doesn't touch my heart.

SPHINXES   It's vanity to brag
                    You've got a heart:
             When all that you've got
                    Is a shrivelled little leather **bag**.

FAUST   (*Entering.*)
             Just to see
                    Such wonders
             Is enough for me:
             They are monsters,
                    But in ugliness
             There can be nobility;
             Perhaps after all,
                    The future
             Will be good.

             Pointing to the SPHINXES.

             Once Oedipus stood
                    Before these,
             The Sphinxes,
             And solved the riddle of man.

             Pointing to the SIRENS.

             And before these,
             The sirens,
                    Ulysses
             Struggled, bound
             To the mast of his ship.

             Pointing to the GRIFFINS.

             And these,
             The Griffins,
                    Stand guard around

The richest treasures
        In the world.

Pointing to the SPHINXES.

You are in the images of women,
        Tell me:
Have you seen Helen?

SPHINXES   The last of our line
                Was killed by Hercules,
            Long before Helen's time:
            Now go away, climb
                Into the air,
            Speak to the feathery
                Creatures there;
            Leave us alone
                To our ancestral duty,
            The regulation of the blaze
                Of the sun,
            The glow of the moon,
            The solar and the lunar days.
            We sit before the pyramids,
            The high court of the human race,
                Watching centuries of war and peace
            With not one change on one stone face.

II. 5   On the Upper Peneus

SIRENS *on the upper Peneus as before.*

SIRENS   (*Sing.*)
                    Dive into the river's torrent;
                    Splash and swim,
                        Singing a happy hymn
                    For all who are in torment.

                    Without water, no well being!
                    Now we'll swim
                        Down to the Aegean sea;
                    What pleasures we will bring.

MEPH   (*In the plain.*)
               Northern witches?
                         Never had a problem.
               The Blocksberg,
                         My local area,
               Is a homely kind of place;
                         Hasn't changed in a thousand years.
               But here?
               It's all mayhem
                         And hysteria;
               You're out for a little stroll
                         And the ground begins to shake,
               It's an earthquake;
               One moment,
                         there's a pleasant,
               Flattish kind of view;
               Next,
                         A mountain's reared up
               Right behind you.

               The LAMIAE *appear.*

               Now, gently, gently,
                         Self-control;
               When one has an extreme appetite,
                         One can bite
               Off more than one can chew.

               Standing still.

               Men have Adam's curse:
               Nothing gets better,
                         Everything gets worse.
               You get older,
                         But wiser?
               Never.
               Infatuation, fascination,
               How many times have I been through this?
               The lure of a tightened bodice
                         With a trim of lace;
               The sweet smile of a painted face . . .
               You want to touch
                         So much,
               Though you know there's nothing healthy

There,
Those luscious bare
  Limbs, they're rotten
Through and through.
But one whistle
  From the lovely hussies
And what do you do?
  Rush right in there.

LAMIAE   He hesitates,
     He debates,
   Should he, shouldn't he
   Be a very naughty
     Man out on the town?
   Quick, attack him,
     Attract him,
   Stick him down.

MEPH.   Don't be a fool,
     Don't be the prey
   In their web; relax and walk away.
   They're doing their job and I'm glad;
   If there weren't any witches
   The life of a devil
     Would be very sad.

LAMIAE   Circle this hero;
     One of us is sure
   To make his juices flow.

MEPH.   You certainly all look a delight,
     Though with the aid
   Of this rather dim light.

EMPUSA   (*Pushing forward.*)
   I want to be like you,
     Please, please,
   Let me join in too.

LAMIAE   You're one
     too many for our coven
   And you're foreign,
   You'll spoil our fun.

MEPH.

If one lives
             Abroad,
One expects to find strangers;
But this place is full of relatives;
From Germany to Greece
             Everyone's a cousin or a niece.
Hello, Empusa.

EMPUSA

Hello, uncle;
             Want to come to bed?
Look, in your honour
             I put on this ass's head.

MEPH.

I know that love in the family
             Is a common Greek custom;
But sleeping with a niece
             Dressed up as a donkey,
Must be rock-bottom.

LAMIAE

It's all pose
             With you;
All dirty talk
             and no do:
Stop the fuss,
             Stop the boasting,
Pick one of us,
             Try the real thing.

MEPH.

I pick . . .

He embraces her and recoils.

A shrivelled broomstick!

Embracing another one.

Ah, something
             Pretty,
And very young.

He recoils.

Ah! Changed into a bee,
             Used her sting

And stung me.
What if I err
      For someone petite
And meek?
Ah! A lizard,
      A streak,
Straight between my feet.
I know what's missing,
      A touch of class:
This fine
      Tall one's for me.
Ow! What am I kissing?
      A prickly pine tree.
I'll risk this
      One last time;
I'll go for a fat one,
I'll relish
      Something warm and wobbly;
Mm, feels spongy
      Like a jellyfish;
I know a Sultan
      Who'd pay a lot for this
For his harem.
      Oh no.
      I think I'm going to scream,
This is worst
      Of all:
She changed into a puffball,
      Then she burst.

LAMIAE   Break away,
      Dart like lightning
Round the witches' son;
You forced your entry
      Into our country,
Whatever tricks we've done
      Are far too good
For the likes of you.

MEPH.   (*Shaking himself.*)
Travel doesn't seem
      To have broadened my mind
One inch. I still find

It as absurd down south
      As it is up north.

Getting lost among the rocks.

Where am I?
      The path was there,
Now it's a nightmare
      Of rubble.
My Sphinxes,
      Where have you gone?
I'm in deep trouble.
It's crazy,
This whole mountain
      Appeared tonight
Out of nothing.
Moonlight
      Has never shone
In this darkness.
But in that bush over there,
      A light glimmers,
A tiny glow . . .
      I know
What it is;
How miraculous,
      Suddenly everything fits;
It's Homunculus.
Where are you going
      Little man?

HOMUNCULUS Floating
      Where I can;
I pass
      From place to place,
Impatient to come into being
      In the real sense,
When I break my glass;
Though, from what I see
      Happening out there,
I don't know if I dare.
But, and this
      Is in the strictest confidence,
I'm on the track
      Of two philosophers

I overheard philosophise:
>> It was Nature this
And Nature that, Nature was all,
>> Nature was wise.
They're bound to know
>> The essence
Of human nature too;
I must find them again,
>> And ask them how to face
Existence,
>> How to join the human race.

MEPH.   No, do it all on your own!
>> If you don't find
Out your own mistakes,
>> You'll never develop a mind.
To exist
>> Is to be alone.

HOMUNCULUS No I'd be lost
>> Without professional advice . . .

MEPH.   Which will be all very nice,
>> I'm sure.
Go on then. We'll see
>> What we shall see.

ACT THREE

III. 1   Before the Palace of Menelaus in Sparta

MENELAUS *enters with* SOLDIERS *and* PRISONERS, *six*
WOMEN IN CHAINS *and* HELEN.

MENELAUS   You women will go on ahead, up to the
>> fruitful fields of the plateau
Where the sacred river Eurotas runs; there on
>> its beautiful banks
Stands my high-towered home; tell the guards
>> at the gate

Who you are, and summon my stewardess and
                                    her many maids;
Do your household duties, inspect the
                                    glittering gold,
The shining silver; then, when you have
                    checked all is clean and in good order,
Take as many tripods, the number you think is
                                    needed
To properly perform the sacred ritual of the
                                    rites;
Pour the purest water into the high-rimmed
                    jugs from the holy spring,
Collect the kindling, dry wood to quickly flare
                                    into flames;
Then, fulfil your final task: to hone the holy
                    blade of the axe.

Exit MENELAUS, *and the* SOLDIERS.

HELEN   I have sailed, longing to be happy, back to my
                              home in my husband's ship;
               Now he sends me to speak to the city as his
                                    herald;
               What is it he wants? Do I return as a wife or a
                                    queen,
               Or, oh horror, as a sacrifice, to pay for my
                              Prince's pain,
               And soothe the griefs and sorrows of the long-
                              suffering Greeks?
               I have been conquered, but am I a captive too?
                                    I cannot say:
               Cut kindling, he said, prepare the axe; but
                              what will be killed?
               Yet I'm happy; here is the palace, the lovely
                              place I played in as a child;
               At last, I am in the home I longed for and so
                                    nearly lost.

               HELEN *in the palace. Sudden night.*

               What's this? Now I'm where
               I yearned for years to be,
               Why do I feel this fear?
               No, fear is a feeling

Below the dignity of Zeus's daughter;
She is not touched by horror's hand;
But phantoms rise in myriad forms,
Born in the womb of the wicked night,
Harrowing even the hearts
Of heroes with the fear of hell.
I saw a woman wearing a veil
Hunched by the hearth;
The mysterious monster
Floated up from the floor;
Its gaunt height, its hollow eyes
Made my mind dazed. Look!
It dares to stand directly
In the light, arrogantly letting
Us see its shape. You!
We women rule here by right,
And soon the king will come.

MEPHISTOPHELES (*as* PHORKYAS)
appears between the door-posts.

CHORUS   Though the locks of my hair look young
                         I have seen many horrors
                In war time; but none as terrible as
                         The night that tall Troy fell:

                Through dust and debris,
                         Through screams of wounded soldiers,
                The great god of discord
                         Roared out his wrath;

                The lick of flames leapt
                         Roof to roof;
                Fire smashed with the force
                         Of a storm through the city;

                And fleetingly, through fog of smoke
                         From burning buildings,
                I saw gods, wonderful figures, gigantic,
                         Come running, shouting with rage.

                Or did I? Or was I
                Fixed with fear,
                Mind-moiled,

And made up the memory?
But I know with my eyes
This horror is here;
I'd try to grab and hold it hard
But dare not, it's too dangerous.

PHORKYAS   It's a common saying, but with a cruel kind of
                                                        sense,
                That modesty and beauty are just not made to
                                                        mix.
                You think I don't know you, you battle-bred
                                                war babies?
                And you, the would-be woman of wild wiles,
                                                man-mad
                Helen, the Hedonistic harpy, seducing and
                                                seduced,
                Who's sucked dry the strength of soldiers and
                                                whole cities;
                I see you all as a hungry horde, a clicking
                                                cloud of locusts
                Swooping down on fertile fields of millions of
                                                innocent men.

LEADER OF THE CHORUS
                How ugly ugliness looks next to beauty.

MEPH.   How stupid stupidity looks next to wisdom.

HELEN   You are rude and insulting, but you rake
                Embers of the coals, memories of the
                                                catastrophe
                Of my life. Is it memory or madness?
                Was that me then, is that me now,
                A dream image of horror, a destroyer of cities?

CHORUS   Be silent! Be silent!
                He comes in sheep's clothing,
                Evil under an innocent fleece;
                You stir up the sorrows of the past,
                You darken the peaceful glow of the present
                You snuff out the flame of hope for the future;
                Be silent! Be silent!
                So the soul of our Queen,
                Which already hovers over Hades,

      May linger a little longer,
      And cling to the form of all forms
      That the sun has ever shone upon.

PHORKYAS   Yes, come out from the clouds, King sun, why
                 not?
      Though I'm spat at and sworn at because I'm
             so ugly, I can stare
      With the best as your beauty blazes in sunlight.
      So, lovely lady, tell me what you want me to do.

HELEN   Stop wasting time with your stupid talk,
      And set up the sacrifice for the King.

PHORKYAS   All's ready; blade and bowl for the blood;
      The ceremony can start. So who's the victim?

HELEN   The king never said.

PHORKYAS   Never, a nightmarish word.

HELEN   You mean . . .

PHORKYAS   No mystery, the victim is you.

HELEN   The king cannot be so vicious . . .

PHORKYAS   These too will be done to death.

CHORUS   Oh hateful horror, oh cruel act.

PHORKYAS   For you it's the axe.

HELEN   Oh terrible, I am a wretched woman.

PHORKYAS   (*To* HELEN, *then to the* WOMEN.)
      At least you'll die with dignity; but for you,
             the news is nastier:
      You'll be hanged, high on the roof beam of the
                house,
      Dangling like dead thrushes, strangled by a
              bird-catcher.

She claps her hands, whereupon masked, dwarfish figures appear at the gate; they carry out the command swiftly, as soon as they are uttered.

Merry monsters, there's delightful damage
To do here! Set up the high altar with the
        abhorred horns;
Set the sacrificial silver, the bowl for the blood,
The axe at its rim! Set the basin for water for
        washing,
There'll be splashing and spurting of black
        blood;
Cast the magnificent carpet down in the dust,
To roll the head up royally, once the royal
        head's hacked off.

LEADER OF THE CHORUS

Stewardess, we were silly, crude and callous
In our words to you; you are a wise woman; we
Beg you, be kind, tell us, can we escape
The crude necklace of the noose
That narrows round our necks?

PHORKYAS There is a man in a mighty castle,
Built by his brave tribe:
They came from the cruel North,
From the impregnable walls they imposed
Their will, plaguing the land and its people.
This man may help you.

HELEN   What is he? A bandit, a Barbarian?

PHORKYAS The Greeks call Barbarians beasts and
        cannibals,
But who were the foul flesh-eaters in front
        of Troy?
This man is a great and generous lord,
Witty and wise,
Kind and considerate;
I trust him, he's good and true;
And his castle! Towering and tall,
Wide as the world,
In its high halls
They dance night and day.

CHORUS   Are there dancers?

PHORKYAS   Dozens of dancing boys with beautiful curls,
                  Smelling of youth, the scent Prince Paris
                  Sweated, when he sidled up to our quivering
                                                          Queen.

HELEN   You're presumptuous, you forget your place.
                  What is your last word?

PHORKYAS   The last word belongs to you: say 'yes' and
                                                  before you blink
                  You'll be whisked to within the castle walls.

CHORUS   Say the word, whisper it, shout it, but say 'Yes'.

HELEN   I don't believe King Menelaus could ever be
                                                  so cruel to me.

PHORKYAS   No? What did he do to the brother of dead
                                          Paris, Deiphobus,
                  Who caught and claimed you, his brother's
                                          widow, as his concubine?
                  Kind King Menelaus cut off his ears, cut off
                                          his nose, cut off much more.

HELEN   He did that to Deiphobus for me, it was
                  rightful revenge.

PHORKYAS   And now his revenge will rain down on you;
                                          beauty cannot be
                  Sliced in two and shared; whoever has it
                                                          whole
                  Would rather destroy it, denying its delights to
                                                          another.

                  Trumpets from a distance. The CHORUS
                  starts in terror.

                  The trumpet's blare tears
                  Ear and entrails,
                  Just as jealousy
                  Claws and cuts
                  A man's hating heart.

Hear? The king comes
To hack off the head
Of his private possession.

HELEN   I have decided; I'll dare
To do this desperate thing;
I fear you embody all that's evil,
You will bend the good into bad.
But I will come with you to the castle;
The rest will remain
Buried in my very being,
None will ever know
The secrets in my soul.
Old woman, show the way!

*Mists are spreading, veiling the background
and the foreground at will.*

CHORUS   Sisters, suddenly
The bright day dies,
Bands of mist blind us;
Are we walking,
Hobbling, hopping,
Falling, floating . . .
Yes, suddenly the sun smears into grey-dark
dimness,
The murk of the mist lifts; brick-brown walls,
Dreary and dank stone; what are we seeing? A
courtyard, a cemetery?
This is terrible place, sisters, we are in a palace
of pain, a prison.

III. 2 Inner Courtyard of the Castle

Surrounded by ornate, fantastic buildings of the Middle Ages.

FAUST, *after a long train of* SQUIRES *and* PAGES *has come
down, appears at the head of the stairs in the court costume of a
medieval knight; he descends slowly, with great dignity.*

FAUST   (*Advancing, with a man in chains at his side.*)
Instead of coming to meet

You with proper ceremony,
I am forced to greet
                You with this servant in chains,
Suffering the pains
For forgetting his duty.
This man,
                Ordered to scan
From the watchtower, the breadth
Of space between heaven and earth,
Did not report he had seen
You approach, oh illustrious Queen;
So the fit reception,
                The celebration
Due to you, cannot happen.
For this crime his life is forfeit;
But you alone
                Shall condone
Or condemn, as you see fit.

HELEN   You show me high honour,
                     Giving me power to punish or pardon;
                     Therefore I'll do the judge's first duty,
                     And hear the accused argue.

LYNCEUS   Waiting for the glory
                                Of the morning to rise,
                                I turned my eyes
                                South and saw
                                One
                                More beautiful than the sun,
                                You, my lady;
                                Your beauty
                                Totally
                                Blinded me;
                                Threaten to destroy me,
                                But isn't anger
                                Soothed by beauty?

HELEN   How can I punish the poisonous evil
                     That I myself make?
                     Why does cruel fate cut
                     My life to pieces, pursuing me,
                     Maddening and bewitching men,
                     So that they destroy all we hold holy?

Demi-gods, heroes, gods and demons
Chase Helen, steal and seduce,
To and fro, to and fro;
My first self confused continents,
My double did more,
Now three-fold and four-fold
I lay misery on misery.
Free this good man from his fetters;
He shall not suffer
Because a god beguiled him.

FAUST   Queen, I am amazed to see
                    One arrow hit
               Both the archer and the target;
               I bent the bow
                    And the arrow
               Lays me low;
               Now *your* arrows fly,
               Their spinning feathers whir
               Down the castle's corridors,
               Criss-crossing in the air
                    On all the floors,
               In all the rooms:
               Defeat looms,
               My men stir
                    To rebellion,
               Now they obey you
               The unconquered,
                    All-conquering woman.
               What can I do,
               But surrender too;
               I kneel; you are mistress
                    Of all I possess,
               You own me, own
                    My castle and my throne.

               LYNCEUS *with a chest and* MEN *carrying
               others.*

LYNCEUS   I will pour
                 All my treasure
                 On the floor
                 Before your Highness;
                 Reason, wealth, power

                    Must cower
                    Before your uniqueness.

FAUST   Take that away; I
                            Am the one who gives her things,
                    Not you.
                    Go, make the castle a new
                    World, arrange its treasure,
                            The loot of kings,
                    In a display of great splendour;
                    Make the grandeur
                    Of the ceiling's vaults
                            Sparkle like new skies,
                    Make an artificial paradise,
                            Bring the lifeless to life!
                    The floor will be a field
                            Of soft gold that will yield
                    To her gentle step;
                    Her eyes shall light
                            On splendour so bright
                    It would blind all but the gods.

LYNCEUS   Happily;
                    For this lovely lady
                    Everything we do
                    Is easy.

                    Exit.

HELEN   (*To* FAUST.)
                    I want to talk with you; come, sit by my side;
                    The empty seat wants its master, and I want
                                                              mine.

FAUST   Queen, give me your hand
                            And your orders;
                    Confirm me as co-sovereign
                            In
                    That land
                            That knows no borders;
                    You have won
                            Guard, admirer,
                    Servant, lover,
                            All rolled into one.

CHORUS   Closer and closer,
Leaning and looking,
Shoulder to shoulder,
Knee to knee,
They caress and cuddle,
Simper and sway;
Majesty doesn't deny
The most private and secret pleasures,
Putting all on public display.

HELEN   I feel so far away,
            Yet I know I'm near;
Oh the peace, the pleasure
To say:
            I am here.

FAUST   I can't breathe
            Can't speak;
My thoughts seethe,
            My head
Spins;
I've entered a dream world,
Time and place have fled;
There is no past or future,
            Only this fleeting . . .

HELEN   . . . Yes, only this
            Perfect moment is bliss.
My life is over,
            Yet I'm living it anew;
But you are a stranger,
            I don't know why
Your life and mine
            Are made to entwine.

FAUST   Don't brood over
The uniqueness of fate;
            The moment
Offers a gate
            To happiness; don't resist,
Open it.
Our duty is to exist,
If only for a second.
You are descended

From the highest of the gods;
You are not intended
To be imprisoned by a castle
                    Full
Of horror;
You belong to Arcadia,
The eternal world of youth and plenty;
That's why you came to my gate,
                    To the brightest fate;
Our throne becomes a flower
Bedecked and shady bower;
                    Now our lives will be
Arcadian, happy and free.

III. 3   Arcadia

The scene changes completely. Closed arbours lean against rocky caves. A shady grove reaches up to the surrounding rocks. FAUST and HELEN are not seen. The CHORUS are scattered around, sleeping.

PHORKYAS (MEPHISTOPHELES.)
                    I don't know how long the girls have been
                                        dozing
                    And whether they saw what I saw;
                    Which was not just Helen and him in the raw
                    Doing just about everything; but another thing
                                        too,
                    That's utterly amazing;
                    I can't wait to tell the girls,
                                        And you lot too,
                    Sitting out there, waiting in hope
                    Of seeing *some* kind of explanation
                                        Of these magical, classical scenes,
                    With which the human mind can cope.
                    Get up! Get up! Prise open eyes, uncrumple
                                        curls and listen to me!
                    In a cool cave
                    Our lord and our lady
                    Lay languidly,
                    On a bed of soft grass; I pass
                    Over the earlier scene discreetly;

Then suddenly there's laughter
Light lovely laughter,
     Echoing around
These Arcadian caves;
And I look, and I see a boy,
     leaping with joy
From the lady's lap to the man,
Mother to father:
The billing and cooing,
Teasing and joking,
Joyful shrieking,
     Deafens me.
He's naked, a faun but human in form,
     A wingless genius,
He jumps to the ground, but the ground
Bounces him back, high in the air; then
     Bounces again,
One, two, and touches heaven.
In his hand he holds a golden lyre,
     Like a little Phoebus,
Son of Apollo;
Out he steps, smiling
     To the edge of the precipice;
His parents delight in their darling,
For what gives the effect
     Of a glow around his head,
Jewels or the flame
     Of superior intellect?
And so his boyish movements and gestures
     Are measures
Of the future man, who will grow
     To be beauty's master:
Through his limbs
     Eternal melodies will flow.

HELEN, FAUST *and* EUPHORION.

HELEN   Love, to make mortals
               Happy,
        Brings two together;
        Then, for divine delight,
               Makes them into three.

FAUST   Then all is easy,

All is fine,
I am yours, you are mine,
It's easy
          And forever.

EUPHORION   Skip,
                    Jump,
             High
                    Up;
             To fly
             In the sky,
                    Higher and higher,
             Is my desire.

FAUST   Be moderate, moderate;
                    Have fun
             But don't get hurt;
             We'd be destroyed
                    If something happened
             To our lovely son.

EUPHORION   I thicken
             On the ground,
             Muscle bound;
             Let go
                    Of my
             Hands,
             Clothes,
             My hair;
                    It isn't fair:
             I want to fly,
             I want to be free.

HELEN   Think of to whom
                    You belong;
             If you destroy
                    The joy
             Of the family,
                    We three
             Together,
             Think how it would hurt
             Your father and me.

EUPHORION   Alright, I won't do

A thing:
Does that please the two of you?

He weaves through the CHORUS, *drawing
them with him to dance.*

Are the steps right?
Is the rhythm tight?

HELEN   Yes that's
                    Lovely,
               Now, lead the beautiful girls
                    In the graceful swirls
               Of the dance.

FAUST   Dancing I can do without;
                    I can't see the point
               In all that fluttering and prancing about.

EUPHORION *and* CHORUS, *dancing and
singing, moving in interweaving dance figures.*

CHORUS   Long hair licking
               Smooth skin of shoulder,
                    How I shudder;
               Bare feet floating
               Light steps swift and svelte,
                    Oh how I melt;
               Manly muscles
               Lithe limbs of a child,
                    My heart goes wild.

Pause.

EUPHORION   (*Carrying a young* GIRL.)
               I'll drag her in,
                    Tough
               Little girl,
                    Whirl
               Her round and round
                    For my pleasure,
               Press her breast,
               Kiss her
                    Unwilling mouth;

Any length
　　　To show my strength;
Make her be still,
Terrorize her
　　　With my will.

GIRL　　　　Let go or you will find
Equal strength of body and mind;
Do you think you can rule
　　　The likes of me?
Fool,
I'll scorch you and burn you
Just because it's amusing to do.

She flares up and blazes high.

EUPHORION　*(Shaking off the last flames.)*
Rock after rock here,
　　　The forest
Presses
　　　In on me;
I hate this nearness,
　　　Narrowness;
Time
　　　To leave home;
The winds whistle
　　　The waves foam,
I hear them,
　　　Far away.

He leaps even further up the rocks.

I must climb a higher,
　　　See a wider
World.

CHORUS　　May sacred poetry
Always fly
To high heaven;
May the brightest star
Shine forever
From afar;
May we hear the poet's song
And see the star's glow

                                    For as long
                          As we live below.

EUPHORION   I'm not a baby;
                    I am a man,
                                I am armed;
                    I will be more than a destroyer
                                Of women's hearts;
                    I join the brave and the strong and the free;
                    Get away from me;
                    Over there
                                The charmed
                    Path to fame starts.

HELEN and FAUST
                    But you've scarcely
                                Seen the light of day;
                    Scarcely been away
                                From home;
                    Now you are dreaming
                                Of dizzying heights,
                    Flights
                                In vast spaces;
                    What about our family?
                    Are we
                                Nothing,
                    Just anonymous faces?

EUPHORION   And can't you hear the thunder
                                Of the sea,
                    And thunder of war booming
                                Valley to valley,
                    In waves and blood, army against army,
                    The lust and the thirst for agony
                                And pain?
                    Death is the rule
                                We all must follow;
                    Everything else is hollow.

HELEN, FAUST and CHORUS
                    Oh horror, why
                    Do you have to die?

EUPHORION   I won't just spectate;

                        I want to share
            Pain and hate.

HELEN, FAUST and CHORUS
                        Daring and danger
            Invite deadly fate.

EUPHORION   Now wings unfold
                        To hold me;
            Don't deny
                        My dream of flight.

            *He throws himself into the air, his clothes
            carrying him for a moment; his head is
            radiant, a trail of light follows him.*

CHORUS   Icarus, Icarus, bravest of men;
                        Misery to see
            Such tragedy again.

            A beautiful YOUTH *falls down at the feet of
            the parents; one expects to recognise a well-
            known figure; but the corporeal appearance
            dissolves immediately; the aureole rises like a
            comet; dress, cloak and lyre are left on the
            floor.*

HELEN and FAUST
            Joy,
                        Then in a heartbeat
            Bitter pain
                        Comes to destroy.

EUPHORION'S VOICE (*From below.*)
                        Mother, stay near,
            Don't leave me here
                        In the dark . . .

            Pause.

CHORUS   (*Lament.*)
            Wild and wilful
            You flew against fate
            Into the net that numbs

All human hope;
Violently you violated
All custom and code of law;
But your purpose was pure,
You strove with strength
For the splendour of success,
Only to fail and fall.

But sing new songs,
Don't bend, don't bow
To fate and failure;
Spring sings from the earth
Of a new birth, new world;
She always has, she always will.

A pause.

HELEN   (*To* FAUST.)
An old saying is proving true in me;
        Happiness and beauty
Can't be one for long.
The bond of love and life
        Is torn;
Lamenting, in pain, forlorn,
        I embrace you one last time;
Persephone,
        Take the boy and me.

She embraces FAUST, *her bodily form vanishes,
he's left with the dress and veil in his arms.*

PHORKYAS (MEPHISTOPHELES)
Don't let go of the dress!
        Demons are already
Unpicking the hem;
        They'd love to have it with them,
A souvenir in the underworld.
The dress
        Is not the goddess
You have lost, but it's divine!
It'll carry you, up and away,
        High as the ether,
We'll meet again, another day;
        But far, far away
From here.

HELEN's *clothes dissolve into clouds,*
envelop FAUST *and lift him up and float by*
with him.

PHORKYAS *picks up* EUPHORION's *clothes*
and lyre, steps forward to the proscenium, lifts
them up and speaks.

Classical Greece,
      An heroic world:
The spark has gone, of course;
      But I don't regret it.
There's enough of the spirit
      Left, what with the odd poet
Wanting to be a laureate,
And philosophers
      Socretizing.
I cannot assume
      To have the talent
For any of that,
But I can rent out
      The costume.

ACT FOUR

IV. 1   High Mountains

Rigid, jagged mountain peaks.

A cloud appears, floating around the mountains, resting on the
peaks, then sinking down to a protruding ledge.

FAUST   I see the deep and barren solitude
                Beneath me, as I leave the chariot
                Of swirling cloud that carried me, high up
                Onto this mountain ridge; and now the cloud
                Is drifting to the East, dividing, surging;
                It changes, billows, wants to sculpture forms;
                And yes! My eyes are not deceiving me,
                I see the image of a god-like woman

In golden splendour, on gigantic pillows;
She shines with light, like Juno, Leda, Helen;
The image sways in lovely majesty,
And now it rises, hovering, refining,
Becoming clearer still; but is this picture,
Glowing with the loveliness of youth
That I lost long ago, just one more trick?
The early treasures of the heart well up,
Bright memory of Aurora, my first love,
That swiftly-felt first glance, a dazzling jewel,
That, when I saw it, outshone any other.
And now the form intensifies and floats
Up higher still, up into the ether,
And with it goes what's best within my soul.

A seven-league boot tramples onto the stage.
Another one follows. MEPHISTOPHELES
alights. The boots march on swiftly.

MEPH.   Now that's what I call
                   Fast progress.
         But why have you come
                   Down here? It's all
         Gloomy, barren rock;
         I know it well;
         It may shock
                   You to know,
         You're standing on
                   What was once the floor of hell.

FAUST   You know
         Your stories and legends
                   Are all rubbish;
         And here you go
                   Spreading them again.

MEPH.   (*Gravely.*)
         When our lord, understandably,
         Banned us from the highest height
                   To the deepest depth,
         We found ourselves
                   In much too much light,
         Cramped up so tight
         That we all began to suffer;

As hell began to swell
With acid and sulphur,
That was no way to live,
Something had to give;
Inevitably, the worst
Happened;
Up became down,
Down because up –
The origin
Of many a topsy-turvy doctrine –
Monstrous lesions
Rent the continents,
The earth's crust burst
And we fell into a pit;
A bigger and a better pit
With exits for flying in the air;
And now we live there,
As Ephesians
Has it,
'Revealed to the nations everywhere.'

FAUST   To me, the rocks lie
Noble in their silence;
I don't ask 'from where?' or 'why?'
Nature created nature
From herself;
The earth was smooth, without feature;
Then she delighted
To pile up peaks
Gouge out gorges;
Throw rock on rock,
Raising mountain ranges.

MEPH.   I don't care
What Nature did;
Though, on a point of honour,
Remember the Devil was always there.
But tell me:
On your cloud-assisted journey,
From the immense space of the air,
When you saw all the world's kingdoms,
Laid out down there
In all their splendours;
Insatiable though you are,
Did you see nothing you desire?

FAUST   One thing, yes.

MEPH.   Let me guess;
                         Something sublime;
                 Since you were so near there,
                 A climb
                         In the mountains of the Moon?

FAUST   Not at all. I believe
                 There are great deeds
                         Still to be done on earth;
                 I will achieve
                 Astounding things,
                         Things of great worth;
                 Suddenly
                         I'm filled with ferocious energy.

MEPH.   So you want to be famous?
                 I can tell you've been
                         With a heroine.

FAUST   I want power, land, possession;
                         Action
                 Is all, fame nothing.

MEPH.   But poets will write,
                         Singers sing
                 Of your glories;
                 Sparking off all kinds
                         Of stupid heroic stories.

FAUST   You can have no part
                         In this;
                 What do you know
                         Of desire in the human heart?
                 Your nature is antagonistic, rabid
                 With bitterness, eaten by acid.

MEPH.   Ah well, thy will be done . . .
                 Best
                         Indicate to me your latest
                 Silly whim and mad fad.

FAUST   My eyes turned to the open sea;

Waves piled up and crashed, wave falling
Upon wave, smashing and scattering over the
                                        flat,
Wide beaches; and that
            To me
Was appalling;
Disorder and confusion
            Drives the spirit of reason
Into a rage;
But then the pattern of the waves
            Began to engage
My attention;
How a wave will grow, then roll
            Back, barely able to reach
Its goal, the beach.

MEPH.   I've watched waves on the beach
                For thousands of years;
            The mechanics of nature bore me to tears.

FAUST   (*Continuing passionately.*)
            Sea water,
                    Sterile and salty,
            Spreads over the desolate mud flats;
            The hidden power of the sea
            Drives wave after wave, that's
                    King of the beach for a moment
            Only to retreat,
                    Its ferment
            A little foam, feeble in defeat.
            What does it achieve?
            The futility! The dissipation
                    Of the mighty power of the ocean
            Drives me to distraction.
            But I dare
                    To think the unthinkable;
            My mind soars;
            The iron laws
                    Of nature
            Will obey me;
            I will conquer
                    The sea.
            It *is* possible:
            Even the full tide

Has to play
Around every contour,
Every little hill;
It makes way
Round every height,
And follows
The hollows
In the mud and sand.
I have already planned
Scheme after scheme,
I will order
The tyrant ocean
Back from the shore
And reclaim the land;
I will narrow the border
Of the mud-flats,
Drain
The vast
Marshes; I will prevail,
I have imagined it
Down to the last
Tiny detail:
Victory over the sea!
I dare you to help me.

*Drums and martial music are heard from a
distance, behind the spectators, to the right.*

MEPH.   That all comes
Very easily.
Do you hear those drums
In the distance?

FAUST   War again.
An intelligent man
Can only hear the sound with pain.

MEPH.   War or peace,
What's intelligent
Is to seize the moment
That will release
Something to your advantage:
Chance
Is a lance;

                    Stab
                              With it
                    And grab.

FAUST   I've told you
                              Again and again:
                    Spare me your junk riddles.
                    Just tell me what you'll do.

MEPH.   The news
                    Is our dear old friend, the Emperor,
                              Stews
                    In trouble of his own making.
                    Remember the whale
                              Of a time we had,
                    Putting false wealth into his hands?
                    It made him a little mad;
                              He thought the whole world
                    Was up for sale;
                    He came to the throne
                              Very young, you know:
                    He thought that the way to run the country
                    Was to throw
                              An endless party.

FAUST   A great mistake;
                              Pleasure is in power;
                    But what a leader desires
                              Must be hidden;
                    Then all he needs
                              To do is whisper,
                    And loyal acolytes
                              Do at once what they are bidden,
                    And all the world
                              Is dazzled by his mighty deeds.
                    That way he will be noble;
                              Pleasure-seeking
                    Is the vice of a vulgar weakling.

MEPH.   Too harsh, too harsh!
                              I admired his relish of debauchery
                    As empire
                              Collapsed into endless anarchy,
                    Brother against brother,

Castle against castle,
City against city;
Just to look someone in the eye
   Was to live or die
As their enemy;
In the churches, murder and slaughter,
   Outside the gates,
The slitting of throats
   Of trader and traveller.
The rough
   Hoodlum ruled, until
A group of men cried 'Enough!
Purge error,
   Save the country,
Restore peace and prosperity;
Let a new emperor
   Take the throne,
And rule for God alone.'

FAUST   That sounds
      Suspiciously priestly.

MEPH.   That's who they were, priests,
     Anxious to keep their fat bellies fed.
       The church first led
     The revolt and it grew and grew,
       To badly rattle
     The old regime;
       So now our Emperor
     Is coming here,
     Perhaps for his last battle.

FAUST   I feel sorry he's landed
      In such trouble;
     He was always good and open-handed.

MEPH.   Let's watch!
      Who knows who will call
     The way the dice fall?

*They cross over the middle mountain range
and look at the constellation of the army in the
valley. Drums and martial music can be heard
from below.*

MEPH.   If your mind is set
                          On mighty things,
                   Make it think!
                   If you fight
                          For the emperor,
                   Sink
                          The rebels
                   And secure his throne;
                   You'll go down on bended knee
                          And receive a gift
                   Of great honour,
                          And what will it be?
                   Feudal tenure
                          Of that vast region
                   Of coast by the sea.

FAUST   Good. I'm sure
                   You've done more difficult things
                          Than winning a war.

MEPH.   No, *you* will win it.
                          You will command,
                   You will be
                          Covered in glory.

FAUST   What stupidity,
                          How can I
                   Command an army?

MEPH.   Luckily, I pay the wages
                          Of violent primeval forces,
                   Three mighty men,
                   Very tough lads to have about:
                          Just give them a shout
                   And they'll help you out.
                   And here they are,
                          Wearing battledress
                   Of different ages.

                   To the spectators.

                   Forgive these ugly little allegories,
                   But like all thugs
                          Down through the centuries,
                   They do mean what they mean.

SMASH-ALL   (*Young, lightly armed, colourfully dressed.*)
                  SMASH-ALL says:
                  You looking at me?
                        Look at me
                  And you are dead.
                  My fist'll be
                        Right out the back
                  Of your head.

GRAB-ALL   (*Virile, fully armed, richly dressed.*)
                  GRAB-ALL says:
                  Why get in a brawl?
                  I've learnt life's lessons:
                  Loot the lot,
                        Spend the lot
                  Then answer questions.

KEEP-ALL   (*Old, heavily armed, without a robe.*)
                  KEEP-ALL says:
                  Yeah, a fortune can be sand,
                        Running through the fingers of your
                              hand;
                  I say sow and reap;
                        Steal to keep.

IV. 2   Foothills

Drums and martial music from below. The EMPEROR's *tent is being pitched.*

COMMANDER-IN-CHIEF
                  Withdraw the whole army
                        Into this valley.
                  If morale holds up and we show some pluck,
                  Our lads will have some luck.

EMPEROR   It'll turn out alright
                        Or it won't, but I hate it:
                  Is half-flight, half-retreat
                        A feat
                  Of arms?

COMMANDER-IN-CHIEF

It is a strategy,
   My Liege,
Of great subtlety;
Every military mind
   Would find
Mountains at the rear,
   Low hills at front,
An excellent disposition;
Advantageous for us,
   Dangerous for the enemy:
They dare not use
   Their cavalry.

EMPEROR

All that is left for me to do
   Is praise you;
Here, then,
   We will stand,
And prove our strength as men.

HERALDS *are despatched to challenge the*
rival EMPEROR. FAUST *enters in armour,*
with half-closed visor; with him are the
THREE MIGHTY MEN, *armed and dressed*
as above.

EMPEROR

This phantom, this 'other
   Emperor',
Who calls himself ruler
   Over my lands,
And head
   Of my subjects,
I will, myself, with my own hands
   Kill and throw
Down into the land of the dead.

FAUST

What can the limbs achieve
   Without the head?
If it sleeps,
   Everyone dreams;
If it is hurt,
   Everyone screams;
If it recovers,
   Everyone beams.

EMPEROR   I am so angry, he can rule
                       My feet;
               I'll have his head
                       As my footstool.

COMMANDER-IN-CHIEF
                       Advance the right flank;
                               The enemy's left
                       Will come up.
                               Now they'll drink deep from the cup
                       Of our young men's courage . . . .

FAUST   This astute young brute's
                       A hero,
               He'll go straight
                       To the fight.

SMASH-ALL   (*Stepping forward.*)
               Who shows me their face
               I'll smash their jaw,
               Cheekbones and all,
                       And draw
               Out their eyeballs,
                       While I'm about it.

COMMANDER-IN-CHIEF
                       Let him join the centre,
                               And engage the enemy
                       Intelligently.

FAUST   (*Pointing to the one in the middle.*)
               He is quick as lightning;
                       He'll grab
               Anything out of the thick
                       Of the fighting.

GRAB-ALL   Never relent
                       From your basic intent;
               To loot the rival emperor's tent.

               SPEEDY-LOOT, *a subtler-woman, snuggles
               up to* GRAB-ALL.

SPEEDY-LOOT   He's my best lover;

'Course a woman grabber's fiercer;
Loot the spoils?
            I'd loot a corpse's boils;
No mercy!
            Forward to victory!

Exit.

COMMANDER-IN-CHIEF
            As I foresaw,
                        The enemy's right
            Is coming up,
                        Charging with their cavalry.
            We will hold fast;
            We will fight
                        To defend the narrow rocky path
            To the last.

FAUST   (*Pointing to the left.*)
            Sir, here's one more, elderly but fit;
                        Can a war
            Be particular about who fights in it?

KEEP-ALL   I'll hold on to anything,
                        Military position,
            Personal possession;
            If I have it,
                        I'm a limpet.

Exit.

MEPH.   (*Coming down from above.*)
            Back there, armed men disgorge
            From gorges,
                        And lock,
            Jamming the rocky paths;
            A solid phalanx, ready for its task:
                        All out attack.

Aside, to those in the know.

            And you're not meant to ask
                        Where *they* came from:

EMPEROR   Just there:
                         There was one knight
               Now there's a dozen,
               Slashing their way into the fight.
               They just appear:
               And sparks are jumping
                         From spear to spear;
               This will really
                         Upset the clergy!

COMMANDER-IN-CHIEF (*Who has come up.*)
                    The alliance you've made with these two
               Revolts me, they smell of sin;
                         It will not do;
               Trickery will never win.
               But nor will I;
                         I cannot complete my mission
               And I return my baton.

EMPEROR   Keep it for better times.

               To MEPHISTOPHELES.

               The baton's not yours;
               I shudder; your company
                         Is as cosy
               As the touch of the claws
                         Of a carrion crow.
               But go,
                         Take command;
               Show me
                         If you can make us free.

               He withdraws into his tent with the
               COMMANDER-IN-CHIEF.

MEPH.   The stupid baton's no loss;
               Actually,
                         It had a touch of the cross.
               In the end, at all the devil's parties,
               Sectarian hatred
                         Gets festivities going;
               There it goes,
               Piling up the dead,

Shrill and satanic,
The agent of horror,
Spreading panic
                As far as the eye can see,
Right across the valley.

IV. 3   The Rival Emperor's Tent

Throne, in a sumptuous setting. GRAB-ALL *and* SPEEDY-LOOT.

SPEEDY-LOOT What do you know,
                First in, after all.

GRAB-ALL   Faster than the fastest crow,
                That's us.

SPEEDY-LOOT Look, gorgeous
                Heaps of treasure.

GRAB-ALL   Oh, the pleasure
                Of grabbing it all.

SPEEDY-LOOT This lovely shawl,
                Was it for his rebel queen?
            Look at the lace.

GRAB-ALL   A star mace,
                Made of steel.

SPEEDY-LOT Feel
                The ermine
            On this scarlet robe.
                I'll use it as a rug
            For my poor bed.

GRAB-ALL   (*Taking the weapon.*)
            One swipe and a man's head,
                Swish!
            But you've got a sack
                Full of rubbish;
            No, don't put stuff back!
            Grab this little chest,

That's best;
They used these for the money
To pay the army.

SPEEDY-LOOT   It's horribly heavy.

GRAB-ALL   Quickly,
Bend down, right over;
I'll heft it up on your back for you.

SPEEDY-LOOT   My back is breaking in two.
It won't hold . . .

The chest falls down and bursts open.

GRAB-ALL   There lies the red gold
In a heap;
Quick, sweep
It all up, go on!

SPEEDY-LOOT   (*Crouching down.*)
I'll fill up my apron;

GRAB-ALL   It's spilling upon
The floor;
There's a hole in it,
Wherever you go
You sow
Gold.

Enter GUARDS *of the* EMPEROR.

GUARDS   What are you doing, garbage?
Think you can rummage
About where you like?

GRAB-ALL   We don't want to hide
What we're doing;
After all that fighting
We've earned some loot on the side.

GUARDS   You didn't fight; you're scum;
Whoever wants to come

Near the emperor,
         Must be an honest soldier:
                  So hand the stuff over.

GRAB-ALL   I've heard the army word
                       For honesty,
            It's 'requisition';
            Saying 'Hand the stuff over'
                       Is your profession.

To SPEEDY-LOOT.

Grab the loot and scoot
         My darling.

Exeunt.

Enter the EMPEROR *with four* PRINCES.
The GUARDS *withdraw.*

EMPEROR   The enemy yields
                       And flees, his flight
            Peters out in the flat fields.
            The empire is restored,
                       Peace and prosperity
            Return.
                       It took a little trickery;
            But in the end we did it alone.
            True, a stone
                       The size of a mountain
            Fell from the sky on the enemy;
            True, a torrential downpour
                       Of blood
            Trapped the rebels in stinking mud;
            But no one gloats,
                       And from a million throats
            Rises the hymn:
                       'We thank you Lord God of Heaven'.
            Ah, the man
                       Of the moment.

Enter the ARCHBISHOP *(formerly the*
CHANCELLOR.)

The rebels go to their wretched fates;
Those who were loyal,
   Will have great estates;
You will be sovereign lords,
Your own, untouchable, high magistrates;
   Distribute
Justice as you will,
Raise taxes, duty, tribute.

ARCHBISHOP Deep thanks, majesty,
   May your reign endure;
By making us strong you secure
   Your own imperial strength.

EMPEROR Now all of you, go away
   Happily,
To celebrate
   This great day.

The PRINCES *withdraw, the* ARCHBISHOP
stays and speaks with great feeling.

ARCHBISHOP I am afraid for you.

EMPEROR For me, at this moment of triumph?

ARCHBISHOP Worldly triumph, but spiritual fall;
   How terrible
To find you in league with Satan.
What of God?
   What of the Pope
And the wrath of the Vatican?
His holiness will excommunicate
   Your empire into hellfire.
Repent!
All this land, where you pitched your tent,
Gaining victory
   By wicked sorcery,
You will donate to holy church;
Then you will, as penance,
   And, of course, at your expense,
Build a great Cathedral on this spot.
I hear, already,
Its bells peeling through the valley,

And – God grant it comes soon –
On consecration day,
            The faithful will swoon
With joy, as you fall to your knees,
            Sealing your popularity
With spectacular public piety.

EMPEROR   Yes. A great work to cleanse me.
Relief
            Rises in me.
I will make a formal covenant.

ARCHBISHOP   I will draw up
            A watertight document.

The ARCHBISHOP *exits but returns at once.*

With such a big church building,
Up-keeping, wear and tear,
            Administration,
Mean ever-rising costs; therefore
The relaxation of all tax obligations,
And a tithe on the spoils of war
            Will be needed;
God's call must be heeded;
Also, to such a desolate location,
            The transport of stone and wood
Must be born by the crown.
In this we seek the greater good.

He exits.

EMPEROR   The damage done,
            The terrible cost:
Because of those damn sorcerers,
            What else have I lost?

The ARCHBISHOP *returns again.*

ARCHBISHOP   Forgive me sire,
            But that infamous man
Was granted the great shore
            Of the Empire;
He will be condemned,

Excommunicated
        To damnation and night,
Unless you hand
Mother church the right
        To tax and tithe his land.

EMPEROR   (*With ill-humour.*)
But there is no land yet,
        it's all . . . wet!
It's all still under the sea!

ARCHBISHOP   We will achieve our aim.
        We will tax
What he can reclaim.
The church can hold its fire.

Exit.

EMPEROR   (*Alone.*)
Why don't I just give away
        The whole empire?

ACT FIVE

V. 1   Open Country

WAYFARER   There they are, dark and strong,
The Linden trees I knew;
After all the journeys I have made,
        All the long
Years away, I'll stand again
        In their peaceful shade.
The place looks just the same:
There's the cottage that sheltered me
When the stormy sea
        Threw me onto the dunes nearby.
I want to see again
The kind and pious couple who found
        Me, all but drowned;
They were very old then,

Are they still alive?
Shall I knock? Call out? I bless
You, I hope you thrive,
And hope your goodness
          Has brought you great happiness.

BAUCIS   (*A little old woman.*)
Dear stranger, please whisper,
My husband's a light sleeper;
He was always a hard worker,
          But at his age it's best
He gets his rest.

WAYFARER   Mother, are you Baucis,
          The woman who, so quickly,
Revived me?

The husband enters.

And are you Philemon,
          Who so bravely
Snatched all my worldly
          Possessions from the waves?
You saved me,
I cannot speak, forgive me;
          Emotion
Chokes me, let me for a moment
Stand and stare
          At the infinite ocean.

He walks forward on the dune.

PHILEMON   Hurry, lay the table
          Among the flowers in the garden;
The shock
          Of what he sees
Will knock
          Him sideways.

Standing next to the WAYFARER.

The wild sea and the shore
          It devastated,
Where you were

So nearly killed,
Is now tilled
And cultivated;
What was once salty marsh
And barren,
A scene of storm and disasters,
Is treated like a lovely garden,
A picture straight from paradise.
Brave workers under the orders
Of clever masters,
Dug channels to entice
The tide's fearsome forces
Into ditches with huge sluices,
Protected by vast dykes;
Where waves once ruled they are kings.
I never thought I'd see
Such things:
Look! Villages rest
In the sunshine,
Field after field, green
Pastures, thick forests.
The ocean can just be seen
As a distant line of blue;
Otherwise, it's a densely
Populated view,
Packed with activity.

The three at a table in the little garden.

BAUCIS   Not talking,
                    Not eating?

PHILEMON   He wants to know more
                    About the miracle.

BAUCIS   Miracle it was,
                    For sure!
              But it bothered me;
                    It was unnatural
              To see,
                    Sort of . . . devilishy.

PHILEMON   But can the Emperor,
                    Who gave him the land,

Be guilty of a sin?
Didn't a herald announce with a blast
Of his trumpet,
                    The filling-in of the marshes
As he rode past?
They set up the first site
                    Very near to us –
Tents, huts! –
Then suddenly, there was a palace.

BAUCIS   During the day
                The workers slaved away
                                    Getting nowhere,
                Collapsing in the evening;
                                    But at night
                Little flames flickered in the air;
                From the sea fiery and infernal
                Floods were flowing,
                                    And in the morning
                There was a canal.
                He is godless;
                Despite all his lands
                                    He wants to get his hands
                On our cottage and our garden;
                He pretends to be neighbourly,
                But it's all about
                                    Throwing us out.

PHILEMON   He's made a good offer, though;
                We can go
                                    To a brand new property
                On the new land,
                                    Almost for free.

BAUCIS   Don't trust
                                    Land that could fill
                With water;
                I'll just
                                    Stick to my hill.

PHILEMON   Let's go to the chapel,
                                    And look at the last
                Rays of the sun;
                                    Then we must

> Kneel and pray,
> Putting our trust
>   In the old God,
> As we do every day.

V. 2   Palace

Spacious pleasure garden. A canal, wide and straight. FAUST, very old, walking to and fro, contemplating.

The bell chimes from the dunes.

FAUST   (*With a start.*)
         Wretched bell! Like the stab
         Of an assassin's knife
              From behind me.
         My empire stretches away
              As far as I can see;
         But I endure
              Slight after slight
         Behind my back,
         Driving me mad with jealousy.
         My splendid estate
              Is incomplete;
         It is not whole, it is not a pure
              Totality!
         I lack
              That cottage and that garden;
         The thought makes me shudder;
         How could I sit in peace
              Under the linden trees,
         Knowing I'm not the owner?

LYNCEUS   (*The keeper of the watchtower.*)
         A great ship, bright flags upon its mast,
         Sails toward us; it tacks,
               It slides with ease
         Through the water, powered
         By more than the evening breeze;
         Its decks are towered
               High with chests, boxes and sacks.

*A splendid vessel, richly and colourfully laden
with products from exotic countries.*

MEPHISTOPHELES. *The* THREE MIGHTY
MEN.

CHORUS

We land on dry land
Thanks to our captain,
Wishing health and wealth
To our owner
And our patron.

*They disembark, the goods are brought
ashore.*

MEPH.

When we went to sea
        Our ships numbered two;
So what do we do?
Come back with twenty.

THE THREE MIGHTY MEN

What? No thank
        You, go
And have a drink?
It's like we'd brought
        Cargo
That stank
        An 'orrible stink.
We want our bit of extra,
        That's only fair.

MEPH.

Don't dare
        Expect another share;
You've had your cut,
        The bank is shut.

THE THREE MIGHTY MEN

That was just funny
        Money;
We want extra,
        We want an equal share.

MEPH.

Why the long face, the gloom and doom,
When you hear of your great fortune?

High reason has its victory;
        The shore has conquered the sea,
Daily, the sails of ships are unfurled
To journey from the new, safe harbours;
        From this palace
You embrace the world.
And on this spot,
        The whole lot
Started;
Here stood the first
        Worker's hut;
The first little ditch was cut,
Down there,
        Where oars now pull
And splash; it is a marvel,
The project of your high imagination
        And rigorous application.
From here . . .

FAUST   Here! The damned and cursed 'here'!
That's what tears me apart.
        You
Are a kind of clever fellow,
        Let me
Tell you: I feel stab after stab
        In the heart, I can't bear to say
Why I feel ashamed, but
        I can't bear it:
I want that old couple
        On the hill, in their wretched hut,
Moved out;
        I want to sit
Under the linden trees
        At ease,
On a fine
        Evening, knowing that they're mine.
I'll build a look-out
        In the branches,
To see in a glance
        Everything I've done,
The human mind's great masterpiece:
        A land
Of plenty, fit for the people
        To live in at peace.
Listen. The chapel bell.

That sound
               Oppresses me
Smothers me,
               As if I'm shut in a musty hole,
A church or a crypt;
The wings of my free-will
               Are clipped;
When I hear that bell ring
               I lose all self-control.

MEPH.   It is an annoying
                       Ding-a -dong ding;
               It gets in everything,
                       As if life is a dream,
               Forgotten between
                       A dong and a ding.

FAUST   Stubborn perversity
                       Can spoil
               A splendid victory;
                       One must
               Be, of course, but one tires
               Of being just.

MEPH.   So
                       Colonise the stupid hill;
               Why do you still
                       Have scruples?
               You should have done it long ago.

FAUST   Go then. Get them out of my way.
                       You know the new house
               They can move into today.

MEPH.   I'll pick them up, then put them down,
                       And up they'll stand again;
               When they've got over
                       The intimidation,
               They'll thank you for
                       Their sudden relocation.

He whistles piercingly. THE THREE
MIGHTY MEN *enter.*

> Come on, there's a job
> > To do;
> Tomorrow the master
> > Will throw
> A sailor's party.

THE THREE MIGHTY MEN
> > We've been treated
> > > Badly;
> > We deserve
> > > A sailor's party.

MEPH.   (*To the spectators.*)
> Lust for land, an old story;
> > 'Naboth's vineyard'
> In all its glory.

V. 3   Deep Night

LYNCEUS, *the keeper of the tower, singing from the tower.*

LYNCEUS
> Born to see,
> To watch
> What's far,
> What's near
> > From the tower:
> The moon,
> The stars,
> The wood,
> The deer,
> > Infinite
> Beauty;
> I like
> It all,
> My life's
> > Been lucky.

> *Pause.*

> But, sometimes,
> The job's to observe
> > Horrors and crimes:

I see sparks flying
            Through the dark masses
Of the linden trees;
The glow's brightening,
            Fanned by the breeze.
The cottage is blazing;
But no rescue
            Arrives,
The old couple will choke
            In the thickening smoke,
They're losing their lives
            In this burning hell;
Tongues of fire
            Flicker higher
To the branches,
            Now the branches
Burn and fall.
Must I see all
            This horror?
Must I be
Blessed with good eyes?
The chapel collapses
            Under the falling branches;
Snake-like, the flames
            Writhe to the tree-tops,
And down below
            Roots and trunks
Smoulder with a crimson glow.

A long pause, then singing:

            What pleased
            The eyes,
            All dies,
            Down long
                        Centuries,
            Treasure
            That gave
            Pleasure,
            All gone
                        Forever.

FAUST   (*On the balcony, overlooking the dunes.*)
               What grief is singing out up there?

Words and song
           Are far too late.
My watchman wails,
           And in my heart I hate
What I have done.
But done it is. Let
           The Lindens be
Half-burnt stumps. A look-out tower
Is quickly built,
           To gaze out on infinity.
And, up there, I'll see the roof
           Of the old couple's new home,
Proof
           That I behaved
With magnanimity.

MEPHISTOPHELES and THE THREE (*From below, in unison.*)
           Here we come, at a lick;
           Quick to say sorry,
           It didn't go exactly
           Smoothly, actually:
           First we banged,
           We knocked,
           Checked the door was locked
           So smashed it down;
           We shouted and threatened
           And then it happened,
           And it can happen
           With jobs like this,
           They wouldn't listen,
           Oh dear yes, oh no,
           They wouldn't listen.
           Right, we said,
           Here we go,
           We do this by the book;
           So we took
           Them by their necks
           And they dropped down dead
           Out of fright,
           Only out of fright, though,
           Only out of fright.
           A stranger, hiding in there,
           Put up a fight
           But it was alright,
           It was alright,

We killed the man,
'Cos you do what you can,
You can only do what you can,
But in the struggle
There was coal,
A whole lot of coal
That got knocked around
On the ground
In this straw,
That kind-of got alight
In the fight with the man,
And it caught fire,
And was a funeral pyre
For the three of them.

FAUST

Why did you ignore
          My order? Why do I
Draw breath?
I said move the old couple,
          Not burn them to death.
Well, no doubt
          You looted their hut.
Now you've got your cut.

Exeunt.

(*On the balcony.*)
The stars are indifferent,
          They just shine;
The fire is dying down, the fine
Ash hangs in the night air.
          A little shudder of wind
Brings the smell
          Of death to me.
It wasn't a crime;
It was a command, rashly obeyed . . .
What's that there?
          The shade of a shadow,
Shadow of a shade . . .

V. 4   Midnight

Enter four grey WOMEN.

FIRST ONE   My name is Want.

SECOND ONE   My name is Debt.

THIRD ONE   My name is Care.

FOURTH ONE   My name is Need.

THREE OF THEM
           The door, locked;
                 Our way, blocked;
           None of us can
                 Go in the house
           Of such a rich man.

WANT   To the well-fed want
                 Is nothing.

DEBT   To the well-fed, and the vastly rich
                 Debt is nothing.

NEED   To the well-fed and the vastly rich and the
                                self-indulgent,
                 Need is nothing.

CARE   But to the well-fed, the vastly rich
                 The self-indulgent
           CARE can call;
                 I'll slip in
           Through the keyhole.

           CARE *disappears.*

WANT   Grey sisters, we must go.

DEBT   Debt will keep near to her sister want.

NEED   And NEED close to her sister DEBT.

ALL THREE   Grey clouds float,
                           The last star
                  Goes out, a cold breath
                           Is in the air;
                  He's there,
                           He's not far,
                  And he's coming . . .
                           Our brother, DEATH.

FAUST   I saw four, and three
                           Disappeared;
                  The name of the one who stayed,
                  Sounded like 'care';
                           A rhyme with the deathly word
                  'Despair',
                  Then did I hear 'Breath' . . . ?
                  A rhyme with the worst word,
                           'Death' . . .
                  Hollow, ghostly,
                           Muted.
                  I've still not struggled free!
                  Can I unlearn all the magic,
                           The spells and trickery;
                  Spells and the incanting,
                  To stand before you, nature,
                           Simply as a man?
                  Can I be
                           A human being again?

                  I was, before
                           I turned to explore
                  Darkness, and blasphemed
                           And schemed,
                  To curse myself and all the world.
                  Though daylight
                           May smile with reason,
                  At night
                  The mind is curled
                           Up in a nightmare:
                  Spectres and ghouls
                           Thicken the air;
                  We return happy from the fields,
                  From work on the great project;
                  A bird croaks;
                           At once, superstitions project

Fears, warnings, signals
　　　　　Everywhere;
We stand terrified and alone;
The door creaks, swings open,
　　　　　And there's no one there.

With a shudder.

Or . . . Is someone already here?

CARE   The answer to your fear
　　　　　　　　　Is 'yes'.

FAUST   Where are you?

CARE   Here to stay.

FAUST   Go away.

CARE   I'm in the right place.

FAUST *is at first furious, then he calms
himself down.*

FAUST   (*To himself.*)
　　　　　　　　No spells,
　　　　　　　　　Don't use a spell.

CARE　　　　　　　　　If the ear
　　　　　　　　　　　　Couldn't hear
　　　　　　　　　My name
　　　　　　　　　　　　Would pound
　　　　　　　　　In your heart,
　　　　　　　　　For I always cause fear;
　　　　　　　　　I am the opposite
　　　　　　　　　　　　Of what you wished;
　　　　　　　　　Never looked for,
　　　　　　　　　　　　But always found;
　　　　　　　　　Always cursed,
　　　　　　　　　　　　But never banished . . .

Don't you know Care?

FAUST   I ran full tilt through life;

What I wanted, I took;
        If I wasn't satisfied
I threw it away
        Without a second look.
Desire, then satisfaction, then desire again;
With force I stormed my way
        Down through the years,
At first, headlong and hugely powerful,
But now more wise and thoughtful.
I've learnt much
             About our sweet
And complex planet;
I've also learnt you can only understand
The here and now, things you can touch;
        Speculation
About life above the clouds
And heaven,
        Ends in futility;
The wise man loves this world
        And keeps his feet
Upon the ground; who needs eternity?

CARE

        To him whom I possess
        The world is useless;
        Eternal gloom
        Comes down,
        Sun doesn't rise,
        Doesn't set;
        He looks normal, yet
        Inside all is dark,
        Success or failure
        Are just a mood;
        He ignores
        What he's lost or won,
        He's wealthy
        But he's starving,
        Caring
        Only for the future,
        But nothing gets done.

FAUST

        I can't listen
             To your rubbish;
Go away! Stop this crazy sermon.
This jabbering

Could turn the wisest man
Into a moron.

CARE

He freezes inside,
Should he come?
Should he go?
He totters
He falters
On life's path,
He can't decide;
He can't remember
The cost
He's paying,
He's more and more
Lost;
He's not sick
He's not in health,
He's a burden
To others and himself,
Breathing
But choking,
Not choking,
But not really living;
And down he goes,
It's an unstoppable
Sinking,
Feeling crushed,
Sleepless
Under the press
Of a crushing feeling
Of helplessness,
Unable to tell
What is happening,
As he's prepared for hell.

FAUST

Ghosts: you've always been
        Destructive to mankind,
Even ordinary days
        You can ruin,
With a haze
        Of horrors and fears;
It's not that easy
        To be rid of demons,
They're tied to us, tightly;

But the despair,
>   The guilt, the distress,
The gloomy power of Care
I will not recognise;
>   I deny that you're there.

CARE
>   You cannot fend
>   Me off;
>   Feel my power
>   With this curse;
>   Most are blind
>   All through life;
>   But for you, Faust,
>   It'll be worse;
>   You'll find
>   That you're blind
>   At the end.

She breathes on him. FAUST *goes blind.*

FAUST   Night
>   Descends even deeper;
But light
>   Shines within: the sunrise
Of the mind.
What I planned to accomplish
>   I must hurry to finish;
All the meticulous planning,
>   Will win the great prize.
But only the master's word
>   Carries weight:
Workers! Seize tools, man the machines,
>   It's late!
I will build new lands;
>   To finish this great work
My mind is worth a thousand hands.

V. 5   The Great Outer Court of the Palace

Torches.

MEPH.   (*In front, as overseer.*)
Come on, my Lemurs,

My botched-up creatures,
Skeletons with bits
Of ligament stitched
On your bones . . .

LEMURS   (*In chorus*.)
We appear
On hand
At once;
We hear
We're getting land;
Here are the stakes,
Long chains
To measure,
But what
They're for,
We forgot.

MEPH.   This isn't a scientific survey;
The tallest of you,
Lie down! Yes you!
Now mark a line right round
Him;
I want a hole,
The traditional hole
All our forefathers knew;
Four sides and elongated;
Isn't it stupid?
You go with one bound
From a great big palace,
To a tiny little hut,
Dug underground.

LEMURS   (*Digging with mocking gestures*.)
When I was young I was in love
And life was very sweet;
All day long and through the night
I danced with nimble feet.

But now old age has stitched me up
And hit me with its crutch;
Into an open grave I fall
And don't go dancing much.

FAUST *comes out of the Palace, groping for
the door posts.*

FAUST   The clash of spades,
        How it pleases me;
The earth gives birth
        To new land;
A border
        Of earth-banks brings order
To the waves, the sea
Is cordoned with a grassy ribbon.

MEPH.   (*Aside.*)
You are only working for me;
        Your earthworks, dams and dykes,
Are merely the preparation
        Of a mighty feast
For Neptune, devil of the sea.
Whatever you do,
        You are doomed;
The elements are on our side;
        When their great storm strikes,
All your mighty construction
        Will slide
Into chaos and destruction.

FAUST   Overseer!

MEPH.   Yes sir!

FAUST   Requisition more workers,
        Thousands;
Bribe them with pleasures,
Use harsh measures,
        Pay, bully, force
Them, they must not stop;
Exploit the last drop
        Of their strength.
And bring a daily
        Report on the course
        And length
Of the great main ditch.

MEPH.   (*Sotto voce*.)
               Not a ditch, a grave.

FAUST   At the mountain's foot there is a swamp,
                    Polluting all we've gained;
               That poisoned bog must be drained.
               Then a million
                    Young men and women,
               Will face
               An active future, on an open space,
               Green and fertile
                    Fields on a green hill,
               Built by the will
                    Of bold and industrious people.
               An inland paradise;
                    Let floods and freak tides snap
               At its edge;
               The community
                    Will rush to fill the gap.
               A thought transfixes me:
               The only way
                    To be free,
               Is to win that right anew,
               Over and over, every day.
               So the brave new people here
               Will face danger together,
                    Through their long lives.
               There they are: a throng,
                    Standing on free ground,
               Happy and free and strong.
               Oh, I say
                    To this fleeting moment,
               You are too beautiful,
                    Stay.

               FAUST *sinks back, the* LEMURS *pick him up
               and lay him on the ground.*

MEPH.   No pleasure satisfied him, no happiness,
                    No success;
               He persisted,
                    Wooing phantoms
               That didn't exist;
               It's all futility;

His last, bad moment
Was utterly empty.
He resisted
        Me, for one last second;
But time has won.
The old man lies in the sand.
The clock stands still . . .

CHORUS   Still at midnight; now the hand
                Falls.

MEPH.   It is done.

CHORUS   It is over.

MEPH.   Over, over?
                The silliest word
I've ever heard.
Over, and pure . . .
                Nothing . . .
Over and nothing
                Are the same thing.
What is the point of this hated
                'Eternal creation'?
To hurl what was created
                Into nothing?
'It's over'. What's that mean?
It's as if
                Nothing has ever been,
Yet it's going round and round in a circle,
Nothingness to being, being to nothingness.
                My feeling?
I prefer
                Eternal emptiness.

V. 6   The Burial

LEMUR   (*Solo.*)
        Who built the house
                Like a filthy hovel,
        With spade and shovel?

LEMURS   (*In chorus*.)
      Dirt is too good to greet
      A guest in a winding sheet.

LEMUR   (*Solo*.)
      Not even a table and chair?
              Where
      Is all the furniture?

LEMURS   (*In chorus*.)
      Sold because of letters
      From his creditors.

MEPH.   Here lies the body,
  As for the soul, if she
      Wants to flee,
  I'll show her the relevant document,
      Blood-stained and sealed.
  Yet sadly, these days
      There are many ways
  Of depriving the Devil of souls,
  Picking holes
      In the legal procedure.
  You can't trust anyone now,
      Even in death.
  The soul used to go
      At the last breath;
  I'd lay in wait for her,
  Mouse,
      Cat,
  Claws claw, jaws go snap!
      And that was that.
  But now Death has lost its clout;
  The soul hangs on
      In that revolting house,
  The corpse, until corruption
      Drives her out;
  And now and then
  I look at stiffening limbs,
  Lusting
      For a morsel of the immortal;
  But it's not the real thing!
  The corpse moves and gets up again.

Making fantastic gestures of conjuration,
acting like a flank man.

Come quick,
      Lords of the straight,
Lords of the crooked gate!

The ghastly jaws of hell open on the left.

Dogs teeth gape,
      From the maw's vaults
Belches
      A raging flood of fire;
Back there,
      In the scalding air,
I see the city of flame
      Eternally burning.
The crimson surf
      Regurgitates,
Surges up to the gates
      Of teeth;
The damned swim madly,
      Hoping for relief;
But the colossal hyena
Crunches them
      In bloody bunches,
Spitting them back
      Into the fire.
Such interesting sights
      To see,
In odd corners;
      So many terrors
In such a space!
You're right
      To give the sinners
A terrific fright;
They think it's a dream,
      They just can't face
That they are where they are.

To the DEVILS.

Come Lord devils,
Glistening with sulphur

From the fiery hole
Of hell,
Reach up your claws and snatch
The fluttering, fleeing soul!

Halo from above, on the right.

HEAVENLY HOST
Bright messengers
Are flying down from heaven
To give
The news that sins will be forgiven
And that the dust
Will live.

MEPH.
I hear
A cacophony,
A nasty tinkling noise
Made by girlish boys;
That kind of music
Makes me sick.

CHORUS OF ANGELS (*Strewing roses.*)
Shining roses,
Opening;
Fragrance
Floating;
Buds,
Blossoming;

May spring be seen
Again,
In crimson and green;
Bringing
Paradise to he
Who is sleeping.

MEPH.
The power fails
The courage
Is gone;
Cowardly cowards,
Idiotic idiots,
Twittish twits;
The devils are reeling

        Cartwheeling,
    The rolly-polies are plunging
        Arse first into hell.

CHORUS OF ANGELS   To what
                Is not part of you;
    Say no;
    To what
                Hurts your inner being,
    Say no;
    If evil won't let you go
                Heaven will defend,
    And, to the loving who love
    To the end,
                Say yes.

MEPH.   My head's burning,
                And my heart and liver;
    Diabolic aches and pains,
                Sharp as the boiling rains
    In hell fire;
    Now I know why lovers
                Moan with desire
    When they're spurned;
    Ricking their necks for a peep
                Of their ex, lying asleep.
    I've done my neck in peeping, too;
                What pulls my head to that side?
    That's the side
                My enemies are coming from . . .
    What *is* going on?
    Have I picked up a bug,
                Some exotic infection?
    I love to peep, though;
                A lingering inspection
    Of sweet young things, with smooth young
        arms;
    What stops me cursing
                Their youthful charms?
    If I get bewitched I'll be a laughing stock;
    But oh the sight
                Of those little rogues,
    I might have a peep, I just might.
    You lovely little things, do

Tell me;
Are you descended from Lucifer too?
So pretty,
So kissable;
Why should I hide
What I feel?
I am at ease inside,
All as it should be,
And natural;
Come to me, come to me, do,
You desirable
Little kittens;
You are so pretty;
Let me have
One more look at you.

CHORUS OF ANGELS

We come,
Don't back away;
We are near to you:
If you can bear to,
Stay.

The ANGELS *occupy the whole stage.*
MEPHISTOPHELES *is pushed into the*
auditorium.

MEPH.   You call us the damned,
But you are the true
Sorcerers;
You are the seducers
Of men and women.
A real
Adventure,
Can this be the future,
The Devil in love with angels?
Fire all over my body;
I can hardly feel
Those burns in my neck.
Stop floating around,
Angels at impossible angles,
All of you, sit down!
Be still, just for a while;
And when you move,

Move in a more worldly way;
And though your seriousness is lovely,
    I'd kill to see you smile,
A lover's look;
    See? Hook
Up the corners of your lips, like this.
You, yes you, the tall
    one,
You I like the best.
    Though that pious look
Out of a prayer book,
    Doesn't suit you at all;
Look at me
    More lasciviously;
And all of you, it would be more decent
    To go about
More in the nude;
They're turning round, look
    At their backsides!
The rude
    Little brats are so appetizing!

Pulling himself together.

What's wrong with me?
    Boils now!
What is this meta-diabolical
    Health
Problem?
Boils, like Job
    All over me;
Job, Job,
    Who looked into himself,
And was horrified
    But triumphant.
It's alright, it's passing;
    The boils are bursting,
The skin's scarring,
The flames of lust
    Burn out.
And, as you'd expect,
    I shout
A curse at the lot of you.

The ANGELS *float up, carrying away with them* FAUST's *immortal soul.*

MEPH.   Where did they go?
                   The brats
         Took me by surprise.
                   They've taken
         The goods up to heaven!
         Right from under my eyes!
                   That's why
         They were hanging around
                   This grave;
         They've stolen
                   A priceless treasure
         From me;
                   The high-minded soul
         That was my lawful property.
                   What can I do?
         What court can I complain to?
         Who will grant the Devil his rights?
                   The fight's
         Over, you've been disgracefully treated
                   And cheated;
         This is humiliating;
                   Effort stupidly wasted;
         Common lust
                   Obsessed
         Me, and I lost
         The greatest thing that I possessed.
                   In the end, it was easy;
         The Devil was defeated
         By stupendous stupidity.

V. 7   Mountain Gorges

Forest, rocks, wilderness.

Holy ANCHORITES, *scattered up the mountainside, sitting in clefts of the rocks.*

CHORUS AND ECHO   Forests sway, rocks weigh
                   Heavy on us; roots cling,

Densely, tree by tree.
Waves splash by caves
Caves that shelter lions,
Silently they prowl
Peacefully around us,
Honouring the sacred place,
The shrine of love
That comes from above.

ANGELS *appear, floating in the higher
atmosphere, carrying* FAUST's *immortal soul.*

ANGELS   This noble soul
                Is saved from evil;
He who strives
                We can redeem;
See, the stream
                Of love
Protects him,
                The blessed throng
Comes to welcome him.

DOCTOR MARIANUS (*In the highest, purest cell.*)
                From here the view
                Is wide and open,
The spirit is rising;
Over there, women
                Drift past, floating
Higher and higher.
The splendid one, shining
                Amongst them,
With her wreath of stars
Is the Queen of Heaven;
I see her radiating
                Splendour.

Enraptured.

Virgin most beautiful,
                Full of true purity,
Seen
                To be holy,
The equal of gods;
Mother so worthy

                          Of all honours
                    Our chosen Queen,
                          Pray for me.

              MATER GLORIOSA *floats across.*

CHORUS OF PENITENT WOMEN
                    You fly in the heights
                          Of eternal realms,
                    Hear our plea,
                          You without equals,
                    Full of mercy.

THE THREE   You who have not abandoned
                          Sinners,
                    Grant this good soul
                          You have summoned
                    Forgiveness,
                          Which forgot itself
                    Only once, sinning
                          Without knowing
                    That it sinned;
                    Let her eternal happiness
                          Begin.

              THE PENITENT, *once called* GRETCHEN,
              close to her.

THE PENITENT You splendid ones,
                          Lower your faces
                    To me in my joy;
                    The soul of he whom I love,
                          Free now
                    Flies up for judgement
                    From above.

BLESSED BOYS (*Drawing nearer in a circle.*)
                    He's growing
                          Bigger than us already;
                    We can't compete
                          With such big and burly
                    People from down there;
                    Once he's won
                          His place up here,
                    We'll learn a lot from this one.

THE PENITENT He is hardly aware
                          Of the new life
                   To which he belongs.
                   Already
                          He is one
                   With the heavenly throng;
                   See, he throws off
                          All earthly bonds;
                   His old body
                          In its heavenly form,
                   In the prime of youth,
                   Steps forward;
                          Grant me the right
                   To teach him the truth
                          And the way;
                   He is blinded by
                          The eternal.

MATER GLORIOSA
                   Rise to a higher sphere;
                          He will follow if he feels
                   Your presence near.

DOCTOR MARIANUS (*In prostrate adoration.*)
                   May every
                          Better nature
                   Enter in your service,
                   Virgin, mother, goddess,
                          Have mercy.

CHORUS MYSTICUS
                   All that passes
                   Is merely a symbol;
                   Here the unwinnable
                          Is won;
                   The impossible
                          Is done;
                   The eternally feminine
                   Pulls us up to heaven.

End.